THIS BOOK IS PART OF TWO SERIES:

COMMUNISM IN AMERICAN LIFE

CLINTON ROSSITER, *General Editor*

CORNELL STUDIES IN CIVIL LIBERTY

Race and Radicalism

THE NAACP AND THE COMMUNIST
PARTY IN CONFLICT

COMMUNISM IN AMERICAN LIFE

Books published to date:

The Roots of American Communism by Theodore Draper

The Communists and the Schools by Robert W. Iversen

The Decline of American Communism by David A. Shannon

American Communism and Soviet Russia by Theodore Draper

Marxism: The View from America by Clinton Rossiter

Communism and the Churches by Ralph Lord Roy

The Moulding of Communists by Frank S. Meyer

The Social Basis of American Communism by Nathan Glazer

Writers on the Left by Daniel Aaron

Race and Radicalism by Wilson Record

Race and Radicalism

THE NAACP AND THE COMMUNIST
PARTY IN CONFLICT

★

By WILSON RECORD

Sacramento State College

Cornell University Press

ITHACA, NEW YORK

CORNELL UNIVERSITY PRESS

First published 1964

Library of Congress Catalog Card Number: 63-18868

PRINTED IN THE UNITED STATES OF AMERICA
BY VAIL-BALLOU PRESS, INC.

Foreword

ALMOST a decade ago the Fund for the Republic asked Professor Clinton Rossiter of Cornell University to set up a large research project on the problem of "Communism in American Life." A number of studies were commissioned—one of which, an examination of the activities of the Communists in pressure and opinion-forming groups, Mr. Rossiter asked me to supervise.

It seemed to me then that the most effective means for discovering how the Communist cadres tried to obtain public support for party goals was a series of scholarly case studies of affected organizations that would treat in detail the evolution of Communist techniques. Some of the studies were to be concerned with groups set up initially as party fronts; others, with organizations, not originally party-sponsored, that the Communists colonized and captured; still others, with groups under siege that beat off the Communists' assault. The resulting volume, *Studies in Infiltration*, will be published by Cornell University Press in 1964.

One area that seemed clearly to need thorough examination was the relationship of the Communists to organizations of Negro protest, notably the NAACP. I therefore asked Professor Wilson Record, whose earlier work *The Negro and the Communist Party* (1951) was a pioneer study in its field, to undertake a case study of the interaction between the Communists and the NAACP. Mr. Record eventually turned in a manuscript of roughly 100,000 words, five times longer, and covering a far greater area, than what I requested. It was obviously a major sociological work, and I felt strongly that —despite the gap that its absence would leave in my book— it merited independent publication. Mr. Rossiter shared my feeling and Cornell University Press was persuaded to legitimize the change.

In a sense this work is more pertinent today than it would have been ten years ago, before the "Negro Revolution." Mr. Record has investigated with scrupulous care the history of the NAACP vis-à-vis American communism, and his book can, I believe, be accepted as definitive on the subject. Moreover, his understanding of the sources and goals of Negro protest provides insight into much contemporary literature on the Black Muslims, the *cri de coeur* of James Baldwin, and the much-denounced "radical invasion" of the South. His examination of the role of the Communists in the movement toward full equality, and of Negro reaction to the party, further confirms the view that the "radicalism" of the American Negro today is nothing more than a radical Americanism. Despite subjection to slavery and discrimination, the Negro has never massively responded to gospels of alienation but has persistently and with incredible patience fought for his rightful membership in the American community.

I am delighted that this work is being brought out as a separate volume in the Communism in American Life series, for I think that Mr. Record has performed an invaluable labor in filling a number of critical gaps in the social history of the Negro in modern America.

JOHN P. ROCHE

Brandeis University
October 21, 1963

Preface

THIS study is part of a much larger, collective inquiry into the impact of communism on American life and institutions sponsored by the Fund for the Republic. If the studies now in process are as enlightening as those already published, the project will enhance scholarly comprehension of a complex phenomenon in a seminal way.

Although the project director and his associates commissioned me initially to do only a brief monograph of twenty thousand words on relations between the National Association for the Advancement of Colored People and the Communist Party of the United States, in time it became apparent to me—and subsequently to them—that the subject merited more extensive treatment than could be given in that space. On my own initiative I prepared a book-length manuscript. Underscoring the need for a comprehensive inquiry were certain signal events affecting both the NAACP and the CP after 1950.

It is necessary that a study of American communism such as the Fund for the Republic has undertaken include an inquiry into the party's impact on and reactions to racial, ethnic, and cultural minorities. Such groups have been prime objects of Communist efforts; particularly have American Negroes been viewed by Communists as a group whose active support was essential to a realization of party aims. It is appropriate that the inquiry focus on the National Association for the Advancement of Colored People, for the NAACP has been, during the life span of the CPUSA, the most important organization in the area of Negro protest and betterment; no Communist plans for American Negroes would be conceivable without taking into account the existence of the NAACP. The response of the NAACP and the CPUSA to each other has been for the most part hostile. The reasons for the hostility become clear as the history of the relationship unfolds.

The methods I have employed in studying the interaction of the two organizations are both historical and sociological. Although there are difficulties in combining the two approaches, it seemed essential, because of the nature of the subject matter, to use both. The formal organization of the material is primarily historical. In Chapter I is suggested a theoretical framework within which the relations between the NAACP and the party can be studied; an overview of relations between the two organizations for four decades, from 1919 to 1962, is then sketched, with emphasis on the disparity of goals and methods. In Chapters II, III, IV, V, and VI the interaction of the two organizations during specific time intervals is treated, as follows: 1919–1928, 1929–1935, 1936–1945, 1946–1950, and 1951–1962.

Those periods were marked by distinct shifts not only in the program of the CP for Negroes but in the party's whole general "line." Although the 1936–1945 period was broken by temporary abandonment of the United Front program from 1939 to 1941, the decade was one in which the CP generally supported the domestic and foreign policies of the Roosevelt administration. Especially was this true for the four-year interval from June, 1941, to June, 1945. In the seventeen postwar years, by contrast, the CP has pursued a course increasingly at odds with the main drift of American political thought and action. One result is that the CP is now weaker than at any time during the past three decades. Its survival, organizationally and legally—to say nothing of its effectiveness as a political movement—is in doubt. Although many broad developments contributed to the decline, they cannot be presented in detail here, albeit there is a growing need for a comprehensive study of the impact of postwar sociological trends on radical political ideologies and movements. So far as concerns the CP, the postwar period has produced some sharp changes that justify the two separate chapters in which they are treated.

In Chapters II through VI fairly standard procedures are followed. For each period the general political and social setting is described. The major shifts in the CP program are reviewed, and their implications for Negroes and the NAACP are outlined. The internal change within the NAACP and its relative strengths and weaknesses are assessed. Then follows an examination of the interaction between the two organizations and the respective responses and modifications of the programs of each. A brief review of all these developments and an interpretation of their significance concludes each chapter. Then in Chapter VII an attempt is made to put the whole CP-NAACP story in historical and theoretical perspective.

Realizing the facts do not speak for themselves, I have not hesitated to pass judgment on the meaning of events; nor have I eschewed the role of prophet in pointing out the likely course of events and ideas in the future. Venturing onto such ground may be dangerous, but it is a risk that a scholar should not expect to forgo.

The five middle chapters are organized with reference to changes in the CP line. Within the NAACP there were also many changes, and one might well ask why they were not used as a basis for chapter divisions. The reasons are these: Internal changes in the Association were much less abrupt than were those in the party. Such changes as did occur led to no fundamental reorientation of policies or practices, although adaptations to changing circumstances were necessary, if sometimes long delayed. There were no abrupt breaks in leadership such as occurred in the CP, even though, as can be expected in any social action organization, internal rivalries developed and factional fights erupted. Finally, although there were fluctuations in NAACP membership, turnover among the middle echelon and local branch leaders was not nearly so drastic as it was in the CP. Therefore, the history of the NAACP does not lend itself to the neat chronological categories so gratifying to the scholarly psyche.

On the whole, the sources of change for the NAACP and for the party were markedly different. Even when both were reacting to essentially the same circumstances—normalcy, depression, war, peace, cold war—definitions of situations and subsequent actions were saliently disparate. However, neither organization could function with indifference toward the other. Almost continuously, but with varying degrees of intensity, there were reciprocating influences, and in such circumstances attitudes were rarely neutral. The actions of one usually had significance for the other: the CP gave much time and effort to "winning the Negro"; the NAACP could not remain unconcerned about the efforts of a revolutionary party to garner a Negro following. In the final analysis one organization could succeed only at the expense of the other.

WILSON RECORD

Sacramento, California
February 1963

Acknowledgments

FOR the past fifteen years racial and radical movements in the United States have been of absorbing interest to me. Colleagues in sociology, history, political science, and psychology have shared that concern. As the citations in this book indicate, I have drawn fruitfully on their contributions.

My indebtedness to the following people must be specially noted: John P. Roche, professor of politics, Brandeis University; Herbert Blumer, director, Institute of Social Sciences, University of California, Berkeley; Charles A. Gulick and Carl Landauer, professors of economics, University of California, Berkeley; John Livingston, professor of government, Sam Ross, professor of history, and Leonard Cain, Jr., professor of sociology, Sacramento State College; and Seaton Manning, professor of social welfare, San Francisco State College. To Alan Covey, former librarian, Sacramento State College, I am obligated for his cooperation in making available many of the documents used in the inquiry.

Among nonacademic people on whose ideas I have drawn heavily are the following: Henry Lee Moon, public relations director, and Herbert Hill, labor secretary, National Association for the Advancement of Colored People; Paul Jacobs, staff administrator, Labor Project, Fund for the Republic; Eric Hoffer, San Francisco longshoreman and political philosopher; Nathaniel S. Colley, Sacramento attorney and regional chairman, National Association for the Advancement

of Colored People; A. Philip Randolph, president, Brotherhood of Sleeping Car Porters; Lester Granger, former executive secretary, National Urban League; Loren Miller, Los
Angeles attorney and newspaper editor; and Jean Welcher,
associate editor, *San Francisco Independent.*

Space does not permit individual acknowledgment of the
many people, in and out of racial and radical organizations,
who permitted interviews, supplied materials, wrote memo-
randa on specific questions, and served as sounding boards
against which some of my tentative notions could be checked.
To the two hundred or more local officers of NAACP branches
over the country whom I interviewed go my thanks for facts
and insights about the organization as it operates at the
community level and for observations concerning relations
between the NAACP and the CPUSA in specific localities, on
specific issues.

To a number of former Communists, Negro and white,
who must remain anonymous, much is owed for a wealth of
information about obscure documents, case histories of individuals and events, and inside versions of the functioning of
the CPUSA with regard to race questions. In an extended
methodological exposition which is too long and tangential
for inclusion here, I explored some of the problems of using
former Communists as reporters of events in which they were
intimately involved. That inquiry was published under the
title "The Sociological Study of Action Organizations," in
the Summer, 1959, issue of the *Journal of Human Relations.*

In seeking information from active Communists, I encountered a hostility which was not unexpected in view of
the Communists' response to an earlier book of mine and a
number of my articles on the party and race questions in the
United States. In those few cases where interviews were
granted I had difficulty in obtaining any data that could not
have been found in the *Daily Worker, Political Affairs,* and
other party publications.

ACKNOWLEDGMENTS

Editors of certain scholarly journals in which I have published articles dealing with racial and radical movements in the United States gave valuable advice. Particularly helpful were the following editors: Mozell Hill, *Phylon: Review of Race and Culture*; Emory S. Bogardus, *Sociology and Social Research*; Katharine Jocher, *Social Forces*; Hennig Cohen, *American Quarterly*; Hilde Thurnwald, *Sociologus* (Berlin); Alvin Scaff, *Alpha Kappa Deltan*; Charles Thompson, *Journal of Negro Education*; and Erwin O. Smigel, *Social Problems*. The critical responses of colleagues to the articles were also an aid in revising and expanding the present inquiry.

It will be quite apparent that I have here made full use of the journal articles as well as of my earlier book, *The Negro and the Communist Party*, published by the University of North Carolina Press in 1951. More than ten years have elapsed since that book appeared, and much has happened in the interim. The present study not only brings the story up to date but focuses on the party's relation to the NAACP rather than on the party's race program in general. Much of the material in Chapter I was published in the Spring, 1959, issue of *Alpha Kappa Deltan* under the title "Some Historical, Structural, and Functional Differences between the NAACP and the Communist Party."

My wife, Jane Cassels Record, a labor economist with research and publications of her own in the field of social reform movements, was especially helpful in relating the NAACP-CPUSA story to recent trade-union history. She developed the last chapter and contributed importantly to the methodology, the organization, and the style of the book as a whole.

Grateful as I am to all who helped, I take full responsibility for the volume's frailties; he who would receive the reward for virtue must also accept the punishment for sin.

W. R.

Contents

Race and Radicalism

THE NAACP AND THE COMMUNIST
PARTY IN CONFLICT

This book is one of a series of studies of Communist influence in American life. The entire survey has been made possible through the foresight and generous support of the Fund for the Republic. All of us who have taken part in it are grateful for this exceptional opportunity to study the most confused and controversial problem of the age and to publish the results exactly as we find them.

Clinton Rossiter

I

An Overview

FOR more than four decades the Communist movement has been a force in American life. Trade-unions, ethnic minorities, churches, fraternal organizations—practically all groups that could serve Communist purposes—have been the object of Communist efforts. How successful the attempt to influence American institutions has been is, of course, a controversial matter. Finding the answer is a difficult task, and unfortunately the search is frequently guided by desire to confirm an already emotionally ingrained view.

For more than five decades the National Association for the Advancement of Colored People has also been a force in American life. Given the objectives and methods of the two organizations, it was inevitable that they would clash; for in the end one could succeed only to the detriment of the other. The conflict, carried on with the varied weapons used by racial and radical movements, is the core subject matter of this book.

No component of American society has received more continuous attention from the Communist Party than the Negro minority, comprising some 10 per cent of the total population. The black man occupies the lowest rung on the American ladder. It is in the Negro community that the American dream holds least luster. Surely, the Communists reasoned, Negroes must be the group most disenchanted with American industrial democracy and most susceptible to revolutionary promise. For over forty years the CP has tried to break what it conceived to be the weakest link in the American social chain, employing first one approach and then another to capture and direct the affairs of indigenous Negro organizations or, failing that, to establish competing groups of its own. The party has viewed racial conflict and unrest in the United States as issues on which a viable Communist movement might be built, not only in America but over the world, particularly in Africa and Asia. Certainly the party's success in the United States depended in large measure on widespread Negro support.

Of the indigenous Negro organizations serving as objects of attack, the NAACP, because of its primacy as an instrument of racial protest, felt the greatest challenge and the greatest impact. What kind of challenge, how much of an impact, and with what final results are questions that this book attempts to answer. These are controversial questions, particularly among lay people. Opinion ranges all the way from the conviction that the NAACP was in origin and has continued to be a Communist Party front to the equally firm conviction that the paths of the two organizations have never crossed. The truth, as it usually does, lies somewhere between the extremes, but not necessarily at the mid-point; its place in the intermediate ranges will become evident from the material developed in subsequent chapters.

The popular notion, most prevalent in the South but by no means confined to that region, that the NAACP is Communist-inspired or at the very least Communist-tinged has a twofold explanation. The first is to be found in widespread ignorance about racial and radical movements in the United States. The second lies in the fact that some whites and most Communists, though for different reasons, have deliberately cultivated the impression that the NAACP and the CP originate from the same sources and are somehow inextricably linked. The Communists have gained from this myth an exaggerated appraisal of their influence and some propaganda support for their claim to be "the only true spokesmen for the Negro people." Concurrently, white segregationists have used the myth of the NAACP's Communist taint as a *deus ex machina* to resolve the contradiction between their insistence that southern Negroes do not really want equality and the open fact of Dixie-grown Negro protest.[1] Moreover, by pinning the red label on the NAACP, white segregationists hope to cripple its effectiveness among Negroes and undermine not merely its acceptability but also its tolerance by the general community.

In all probability the motives of such whites are mixed. The NAACP, to the extent that it is successful, poses an increasing threat to those whose social and psychological security is bound intimately to the present biracial order. The NAACP and new protest organizations, such as Martin Luther King's Southern Christian Leadership Conference, have challenged the specific instruments as well as the larger ideology of white supremacy, whose defenders, in spite of some momentary success, are fighting, as they themselves seem to realize, a losing struggle.[2] Some of them are willing, as were their forebears, to harvest the "bitter fruits of bitter-endism." In such circumstances what men want to believe and not what the facts allow —what they must believe and not what the legitimate evidence supports—becomes the shaper of action. Involved is not a mere threat to the old restrictions on Negro voting, education, housing, and employment, but a challenge to the white man's basic self-image and to the larger social system of which he is a part.[3]

[1] Jane Cassels Record, "The Red-tagging of Negro Protest," *American Scholar*, XXVI (Summer, 1957), 325–333.

[2] Jane Cassels Record, "Desegregation Near the Bottom Rung of the Ladder," *Antioch Review*, Spring, 1956, 23–33.

[3] Lewis M. Killian, "Consensus in the Changing South," *Phylon*, XVIII (Spring, 1957), 107–117.

Thus it might have been expected that defenders of discriminatory racial patterns in the United States, especially in the South, would invoke on an unprecedented scale the unfavorable image of communism in an effort to justify to others, and perhaps more importantly to themselves, those patterns of anti-Negro sentiment and behavior that violate their political, ethical, and religious creeds. Guilt and aggression are not unrelated, and the white South, particularly in recent years, provides a classical case for their association.[4]

So long as the NAACP in the rural South existed primarily in the private thoughts of individual Negroes who anonymously sent small contributions to the national office and read *Crisis* by lamplight in their homes; so long as NAACP meetings were held infrequently and quietly, in village churches; so long as NAACP activities in the cities were limited and "respectable," consisting for the most part of negotiation with white leaders; so long as the NAACP requested modest privileges instead of demanding basic rights, the organization was "allowed" to exist. With the rising militancy of southern Negroes in all walks of life, however, a development which the NAACP encouraged and organized, hostile toleration was no longer an effective white response. Its place was taken by strident— and if there was sufficient provocation, even violent—insistence that the organization be destroyed by one means or another. One widely employed method was to charge that the NAACP is "Communist," "Communist-inspired," "Communist-led," or "Kremlin-directed."[5]

Ignored is the fact that if the NAACP were Communist, rather than an organization which the CP has tried alternately to de-

[4] Seymour Lipset, "The Radical Right," *British Journal of Sociology*, II (1955).

[5] See speeches by Representatives Gathings of Arkansas and Forrester of Georgia, *Congressional Record*, CII (Feb. 23, 1956), 2797–2848.

stroy or capture, it long since should have gone the way of other party organizations, either passing from the scene entirely or degenerating into an isolated gathering of the faithful few. The intense opposition of whites to the NAACP and to the more spontaneous expressions of Negro discontent in the South today is evidence not so much of the Association's weakness as of its strength, not of its failure but of its success. During a period in which the Communist Party has lost most of its following and amounts to little more than a pariah element on the American scene, the NAACP's voice is steadily growing stronger and clearer.

Although the NAACP has been under attack in the southern states, particularly in Arkansas, Alabama, Texas, and Louisiana, it has maintained its structure intact, held much of its older membership while acquiring new recruits, and broadened its program. Simultaneously it has shown ability to form rewarding associations with other agencies of social change: trade-unions, political parties, religious organizations, fraternal groups, and philanthropic institutions. Its strength has been augmented neither by the recruitment of Communists, which the NAACP specifically prohibits, nor by alliances with Communist or "front" organizations, which the NAACP, as a matter of national and branch policy, has specifically eschewed. Although the present membership of the NAACP ranges the political spectrum, few adherents are in the red band.

It would be rewarding to explore in detail the sociopsychological dimensions of the behavior of those seeking to maintain racial segregation by positing an umbilical attachment between the NAACP and the CP, but that is not the central concern of this study. The primary concern here is the nexus itself, to the extent that it has existed. No matter what approach is made, the evidence points conclusively in one direction, namely, to the basic incompatibility of the two groups during their entire careers. When historical and sociological methods are focused on the relationship, they produce no disparate conclusions, only different and complementary emphases.

The NAACP and the CP have markedly different historical roots. The former was organized in 1909, eight years before the Bolshevik Revolution and a decade before the tortured birth of the CPUSA. Moreover, the NAACP's ideological and organizational antecedents go back even further—to the Niagara, convention, and abolition movements, not one of which was grounded in comprehensive socialist philosophies or led by people with binding commitments to either a socialist or a Communist international apparatus. In 1909 the goals of the NAACP were—as they remain today—quite modest by Communist standards; achievement for Negroes of those rights and responsibilities generally available to other citizens of the United States would scarcely have stirred Lenin to enthusiasm.

Of equal significance is the fact that there has been no basic departure from the methods originally embraced: gradualism rather than revolution, nonviolence rather than force, legalism rather than direct action. In its choice of methods the NAACP has followed the pattern of most racial and ethnic movements struggling toward equality. Certainly the NAACP has never envisioned a fundamental reorganization of American society, apart from racial issues. Because it has developed no blueprint for restructuring American institutions in accordance with a distinctive, comprehensive image of human nature, history, or society, the NAACP may be described as nonideological. Indeed, liberal-humanist critics have commented acidly upon the fact that the organization and its leaders demand no more for Negroes than integration into a white society which from the liberal-humanist view leaves much to be desired.

NAACP goals and methods are radical only in the sense that

they present a challenge to the roots of biracialism and the institutionalized practices of segregation and discrimination, which have been fundamental in American history. In other words, all NAACP objectives could be achieved without disturbing much of the underlying structure of American life: the capitalist industrial order need not be significantly affected; political divisions and values need not be greatly modified; large-scale and ever-expanding bureaucracy in both public and private areas might continue; general educational patterns, geared mainly to supplying occupational specialists and professionals, would not necessarily be altered; and so on. This is not to say that individual Negro leaders are unaware of and unconcerned about American frailties; it is merely to stress the fact that the NAACP is a single-purpose organization, whose only goal is full integration of Negroes in American life, whatever that life may be. Reform of American society along other than racial lines is, in the view of the NAACP, the task of other movements.

Thus the attainment of NAACP aims would seem to portend not an increasing radicalism but a growing conservatism, for to the extent that Negroes share in what they regard as the benefits of the American establishment, they have a stake in its preservation. Those who want to supplant American society will hardly choose the NAACP as their instrument. Nor will the Association be the choice of Negroes who wish to separate from American society, the recent development of the Black Muslim movement being eloquent testimony to that fact.

Compared to the NAACP, the Communist Party was a late arrival on the American scene. Organized and led primarily by first- and second-generation immigrants whose old-world ties were strong, it had few native roots, although it tried, as some students have overemphasized, to align itself with native radical traditions and organizations. From the very outset the

7

CPUSA was Soviet-oriented and Soviet-controlled, although it was not until the Sixth World Congress of the Communist International in 1928 that the CPUSSR finally eliminated the sharp factionalism in the American section and made of it a disciplined adjunct to the larger apparatus. "Stalinization" having thus been effected, the CPUSA forfeited any semblance of grass-roots ferment, surrendering its already limp autonomy with little protest.

It was not until the deep crisis of the capitalist order in the 1930's that the party was able to attract a significant following or to project its influence into non-Communist organizations such as the trade-unions. Moreover, that achievement came at a time when the party focused largely on day-to-day issues and soft-pedaled revolutionary aims. The attachment of many members of that era was to the new line rather than to the party itself. Publicly the Communists called for a pragmatic solution of immediate economic and social problems rather than for a root-and-branch demolition of the bourgeois order. In the international sphere the Communist rallying cry was to defeat a rising fascism, a goal which appealed to a great many people sickened by the new barbarism and eager to act against it. Having little understanding of the CP's structure and ultimate goals and failing to comprehend the party's role as an instrument of the CPUSSR, many well-meaning people gave the organization support and respectability that it could not otherwise have attained. The responses were in large part genuine—and generous. Naïve from the perspective of subsequent history and shockingly betrayed by the Communists themselves, the party's recruits of the 1930's were creatures not so much of an alien ideology as of a native radicalism, which has recurred in American history during times of stress. In other words, during the Great Depression the CP, by adopting an ameliorative rather than an ideological line, was able to co-opt some of the grass-roots protest endemic to American economic crisis. Although its genealogical researches were industrious, the CP never succeeded in establishing more than a distant-cousin relationship with Paine, Jefferson, Jackson, Lovejoy, Lincoln, and Frederick Douglass. From the left, the Communists' claims to be the legitimate heirs of Marx were just as forcefully challenged, but that is another story.

In their efforts to reinterpret the American past and invoke the blessing of American history for the Communist tactical program, the CP researchers uncovered and emphasized aspects of agrarian, labor, and racial movements largely neglected by guild historians. With respect to Negroes and Negro movements, however, party writers siphoned from a reservoir already filled by Negro historians such as W. E. B. Du Bois and Carter G. Woodson. No new viaducts were built, no new springs discovered. The main effort was to try to change the color of the water. The NAACP, on the other hand, though realizing that a viable protest movement required an appreciation of the Negro past as a source of Negro self-respect and race pride, was not compelled to commit atrocities on historical data and historical judgments. Its continuities with the past were uncovered, not manufactured.

If one turns to organizational characteristics of the NAACP and the CP, he finds that there, too, differences are sharp. Both groups, of course, display those general features which are typically found in social action organizations: formal goals, formal structures, more or less explicit philosophies, divisions of responsibility, internal allocations of power, systems of communication, and informal relations among top leaders. However, when those traits are examined in specific contexts, striking variations emerge and suggest a difference in kind as well as in degree. Why? There are several reasons: the NAACP plays by rules which the democratic tradition has set, seeks its goals within their limits, and accepts their validity

9

for internal procedures as well as for outward action. As one observer phrased it, "The NAACP is unusual in that it is carrying out a revolution in the name of and with the instruments of law and order." On the other hand, the CP has always regarded the rules of the game as obstacles to be overcome or circumvented, or as instruments to be used against the political community itself when it is advantageous to do so.

In terms of size the NAACP is an impressive organization, now having more than 350,000 members. Local programs are carried out through more than 1,400 branches scattered across the nation and grouped in state and regional conferences. Local officers are selected by the membership. Although much formal power over branch organizations is vested in the national office and the Executive Board, it is employed sparingly and usually only as a last resort. National leaders try to influence local branch officials, of course, but the instruments are mostly those of persuasion and education. Even if financial and political pressures were applied, there would be little likelihood of their success because of the loose structure of the organization and the dependence of the central headquarters on local leaders. Indeed, the NAACP would be in a better position to forestall the machinations of political cliques and parties within its ranks if local branch autonomy were limited more than it now is. Yet there is still much complaint that power is too centralized at the top. The highly authoritarian internal structure of the Black Muslim movement may appeal to certain types, but the character of the NAACP is such as to preclude recruitment of those Negroes responsive to the Muslim type of organization.

In the branches officials usually hold office for one year. They may be reelected indefinitely. The greatest danger, however, is not that one individual faction will become permanently entrenched but that experienced leaders will not seek office again and carry the responsibilities for which they usually lack both time and money. Absence of able local leadership, especially in smaller communities, is probably the greatest functional weakness of the NAACP; it is likely to continue for a long time, in spite of the training programs of the national office. Even such elementary tasks as keeping membership lists, collecting dues, arranging regular meetings, and staffing key committees are frequently neglected.

Although the national office, headed by the executive secretary with a small professional staff, which is hard to recruit and retain, issues directives and suggestions and provides limited technical and financial assistance, there is a high degree of local choice of issues and methods of action. Of course, broad general rules must be followed, but they are highly flexible and almost any program for Negro betterment can be subsumed under them. In recent years there has been some tightening of policies concerning cooperation with other organizations, a result in no small part of the need to prevent joint ventures by local branches with extremist political groups, particularly with Communists and Communist sympathizers. In this course the NAACP has followed slowly and with some admitted reservations policies similar to those of trade-unions and other minority organizations. Its concern for internal democracy and for consistency in its commitment to civil rights and civil liberties have served as brakes.

White membership in the NAACP is low, declining proportionately over the years to the point where it is now probably less than 5 per cent of the total. In the southern and border states only a handful of whites have joined. With the relative decline in white membership and the emergence of more able Negro leaders, white influence internally has diminished. From the outside, however, influence by trade-unions, political parties, religious organizations, and other minority groups has increased, as a result of the NAACP's effort to develop effective alliances for mutual concerns. Although those obligations have given the NAACP less freedom of action, they have increased its speed toward the goals it shares with cooperating organizations, which have also provided psychological and institutional support generally, apart from specific goals and techniques.

Not only has the number of Negroes in the NAACP increased, but the base has been broadened. Although the backbone of the organization is still the Negro professionals—doctors, lawyers, ministers, and civil servants—more skilled and semiskilled workers as well as better-paid service people have joined. The recruitment of more Negro women and older Negroes has given local branches a group of members with leisure time that can be spent in volunteer work. For an organization that only rarely can finance a regular local office or paid executive this is a welcome development. Further, in turning to other than middle-class Negroes, the NAACP has found new sources of funds.

Again by contrast, the Communist Party is essentially an authoritarian, totalitarian organization, a miniature of the larger social order it would almost certainly establish if its goals were achieved. Local autonomy is unknown; "incorrect" actions and philosophical "deviations" are dealt with summarily, frequently at the cost of party effectiveness. Control is centered at the top, an expression of an elitist concept of leadership which holds that the mass of people, even rank-and-file party members, are instruments to be used by those with a superior understanding of Marxism-Leninism. That kind of organization reduces, if it does not eliminate altogether, the chance to hold leaders to account on the basis of measured performance, such as may take place in a democratic organization; for there is no satisfactory scale on which "superior understanding" and performance can be weighed. There is a gauge, of course, but it is primarily a function of power;

12

the reference points are not membership needs but the vested interests of the elite.

In the CP, expulsion, character assassination, and physical violence are approved weapons. Although they may be employed occasionally in nontotalitarian organizations, their use is exceptional; certainly they are not regarded as standard devices whose mastery is applauded. Concealment of identity, semantical distortion of final aims, deception of insiders as well as outsiders, and studied destruction of individual sensibilities are commonplace practices in the CP. Adherence to a party "line," however fluctuating, is demanded, along with loyalty to the organization as a whole under all circumstances; such total loyalty leaves no room for other commitments, except instrumental ones, to outside groups and individuals.

Communist Party leaders are usually dedicated people whose involvement, if continued, comes to constitute a way of life. They are not selected in response to local group preference or decisions of representative national conventions, as is the case in the NAACP. Within the Communist organization advancement or demotion is dictated from the top—frequently from the outside, if the leaders of the CPUSSR and the Communist International apparatus choose to intervene to that extent. Intraparty fights, such as occurred between Browder and Foster in 1945 and later between Gates and Foster, do not really center on issues that can be resolved through public debates and appeals to members. They are disposed of by quite different means, primarily by CPUSSR intervention through behind-the-scenes agents. Achieving and holding a party position of any consequence, however, is not contingent solely on demonstrated loyalty to the organization under any and all circumstances; technical skills—in speaking, writing, administration, and manipulation—are also necessary. In other words, a totalitarian mentality is necessary but not sufficient.

13

That many party joiners have found acceptance of such leadership principles difficult offers a partial explanation for the relatively high rank-and-file turnover. The absence of internal democracy, clearly indicated in the manner of choosing leaders, is an alienating force for new recruits who desire some minimum autonomy in local activities. Consequently there is a continuing winnowing process, and those who remain over the years will be found to have a marked predisposition for highly structured, authoritarian relationships. In this connection one notes that the declining CP in the United States is composed increasingly of older people, a fact frequently lamented by party spokesmen; efforts to "win the younger people" in recent years have been salient failures. Even some of the older remaining members might sever their connections if they could face the loneliness of the later years without an organization that has so strongly shaped and directed their lives.

Finally, as was suggested before, the CP structure cannot be understood unless it is viewed as an integral part of a larger apparatus. This is the root fact on which any examination of its career, particularly since 1930, must be predicated. Subordinated to the Communist International apparatus, the CPUSA has little discretion in selecting either goals or methods. Perhaps the most dramatic example is its adoption of the "Self-Determination in the Black Belt" program following the Sixth World Congress in 1928. A later example is the repudiation of Browder and his "revisionism" immediately after World War II. Both events will be discussed in subsequent chapters, for they had an important bearing on the CP's relation to the NAACP.

The Association's commitments are of a different order; they stop "at the water's edge," and its leaders do not need to scan foreign skies for a sign of what they should think or what they should do. This does not mean that the NAACP is concerned exclusively with domestic race issues. Through the years its leaders have recognized that the color question is worldwide, just as in the United States it is nationwide. They have perceived that the fate of Negroes in this country is not unrelated to the fate of dark-skinned people over the world. Although no effective organized expression of that point of view has yet appeared, cooperative ventures with Negro organizations in other countries, particularly those in Africa, almost surely will be undertaken in the years ahead. For the development of a global view of color the Communists can justly claim some credit, although Du Bois, one of the NAACP founders, insisted more than forty years ago that Negroes over the world were inextricably linked and proposed specific organizations to implement the relationship. Today domestic black nationalism is given continuous stimulus by African developments, particularly by the emergence of the new African states.

In still other respects the NAACP and the CPUSA are significantly different. Like the party, the NAACP has both immediate and long-term objectives, of course. Day-to-day issues, including housing, voting, education, and employment, are acted upon by various means, primarily legal and political. However, ultimate objectives are much less specific than those of the party; they are expressed in such general principles as "equality of opportunity," "equal rights," and "full citizenship." Members see those goals in ideal terms, as characteristics of a moral and political order they wish to see established. As Charles R. Lawrence has indicated,[6] such slogans may serve as myths to sustain Negroes in their present predicament, just as images of Jordan once sustained their ancestors under slavery. But slogans do more: they invoke the model of a new human arrangement toward which the

[6] "Negro Organizations in Crisis" (unpublished Ph.D. dissertation, Columbia University, 1953).

Negro must struggle; they give a deeper meaning to seemingly pedestrian efforts to realize immediate goals. In such circumstances, and as barriers do crumble, ultimate objectives may seem quite real indeed.

The NAACP, like the American labor movement, is essentially pragmatic rather than ideological. It demands "more, more, and more" without raising very many questions about the ultimates. Getting what is possible in the immediate future is the primary concern. If it failed to emphasize that objective, the NAACP could count on little support from American Negroes. Such an orientation appeals to colored Americans who, like their white counterparts, have always wanted the good society, vaguely defined, but are willing to settle for something less, at least for the time being. Thus the NAACP program is cast in a native, pragmatic mold.

There is, then, no compulsion to reconcile day-to-day demands on the white social order with an over-all ideology or, as in the case of the CP, with the self-defined needs of a larger, international apparatus, capable of imposing its will on its satellites. As NAACP membership is broadened, additional objectives are placed on the action agenda. A good example is the establishment in the West Coast region of a credit union that provides some members a chance to invest savings (with good returns) and other members a chance to borrow money (at reasonable rates). Radical ideologists are wary of establishing such capitalist, interest-charging, pay-collecting institutions lest by their success they vitiate doctrinal purity, but the NAACP's involvement in such experiments is likely to grow as new members with varying concerns join. Furthermore, the need to reconcile conflicting interests through compromise is likely to become greater, requiring greater flexibility in action programs.

Although the concerns of NAACP members may be varied, they do have much in common. From the organization comes a sense of community, a feeling of belonging to a group of their own which can be a source of personal dignity and racial solidarity. Moreover, the organization itself tends to be at one with many other agencies in the Negro community —churches, fraternal organizations, and trade-unions—with which the NAACP can cooperate in joint endeavors or to which it can appeal for support. This compatibility is strengthened by local committees working specifically with each type of institution and by national secretaries handling relations with religious, labor, women's, and youth groups. Rarely has the NAACP been posed against the major institutions of the colored community.

In contrast, the CP displays, with its more elaborate ideology, a smaller flexibility. Its actions must always be interpreted as consistent with ultimate revolutionary aims, a fact which leads to considerable strain in developing doctrinal sanction for specific moves and strips the gears when abrupt acceleration or reversal is necessary. Success in the short run may produce unexpected results which dilute revolutionary fervor and spark organizational dilemmas; partial achievement on pragmatic issues may be as disturbing to the leaders as are abysmal failures.

The dilemma becomes more understandable when one remembers that the Communist program is not intended to meet membership needs as such but to support the world movement whose success is thought to be inseparable from the continued growth of Soviet power and the CPUSSR. No limited objectives are good in themselves; they are means or steps to something else; every action must be so interpreted; self-congratulation is *verboten;* and any hard-won accomplishment is always piecemeal, unless it is the final realization of power. Understandably, it is hard to motivate very many Americans to act with continuing emotional fervor, albeit they are assured that the stars in their courses are with them.

In such circumstances the party tries to define personal needs as coextensive with party necessities, a process in which it is hoped the "I" will become indistinguishable from the "we," the party. In practice, however, the CP has found that the commitment of all but a few hard-core adherents is partial and frequently situationally determined. Indoctrination and expulsion are the principal instruments for trying to deal with such tendencies.

Unrestrained by commitment to democratic rules or pluralist orientation, the party has sought to penetrate as many areas of community life as possible, selecting them in terms of a rank order of importance. Claiming to have all the answers to all the questions and to have them all the time, it has had no hesitancy in prescribing the appropriate goals for every segment of society and for every social group. If it has not been successful, and in most cases it has failed rather miserably, the reason does not lie in any self-doubt about its omniscience. Among the groups the party has selected to receive its gospel are racial and ethnic minorities, industrial workers, trade-unionists, sharecroppers, tenants, artists, and assorted intellectuals. No group in this country has been worked over more diligently with poorer results than have Negroes, only a few of whom were led to discern that their ultimate welfare in rural Alabama required support of the Jewish Soviet in Birobijan. That the CP would decide to concentrate such energy on American Negroes is not surprising; that it would continue to do so in the face of such marked failure is.

The failure was due in part to the basically open character of American society, where alternate ideologies, a heterogeneous population, and a multiplicity of relatively autonomous secondary associations—racial, religious, ethnic, economic, and political—make it difficult for a totalitarian party to recruit a following or to hold it for very long. The Communists' best chances lay in those situations in which factional struggles have become so intense as to destroy faith in the efficacy of the system and in the rules of the political community. Recognizing that, the Communists, while proclaiming the contrary publicly, embraced the necessity of conspiracy, fraud, deception, violence, and subversion as weapons in the struggle for power; they could not likely attain it in any other way.

In the Communist view autonomous associations such as the NAACP have no intrinsic value. They may be historical necessities but, like other historical phenomena, are doomed to pass from the scene. The party, of course, has tried to speed up that process by undermining and sapping or, where feasible, by frontal attack. In their efforts the Communists tolerate no dissent in their own ranks at the same time they are trying to sow dissent in the ranks of other organizations. The fact that the latter are pledged at least to try to accommodate internal opposition, as in the case of the NAACP, provides opportunity for the Communists to employ the weapons mentioned above. What is perhaps most significant about the NAACP's response to the Communist effort is its essential retention of the democratic ethic and of the specific safeguards necessary to its realization.

The major differences—historical, ideological, and structural—between the two organizations provoke fundamental incompatibilities; the relations between them have been antagonistic at root. The party, if one may judge from its actions, regards the NAACP as an implacable enemy which must ultimately be destroyed. When the party was strong, most NAACP leaders viewed it with equal enmity. Now the NAACP focuses on more realistic threats—the White Citizens Councils, for example.

Any organization recruiting members to carry out collective action through democratic means risks penetration, control, capture, or destruction by a disciplined minority with ulterior objectives. In the United States trade-unions, fraternal groups, professional associations, and racial organizations have been tempting fruit for the CP. In some cases the Communists were able to infiltrate and influence such groups. Sometimes they managed to secure *de facto* control although they had little formal power. In still other instances the initial penetration led to capture of organizations and conversion of them to party purposes. Where capture proved impossible, the Communists did not hesitate to destroy the association outright if they could. Some examples: the National Lawyers Guild was penetrated; the National Maritime Union was controlled; the Southern Negro Youth Congress was captured; the National Negro Congress was destroyed.

Because of its importance in racial protest and because Negroes were a prime target for the CP, the party tried every tactic on the NAACP at one time or another. Lawrence has noted that:

> In common with many other social action agencies the N. A. A. C. P. has felt the threat of Communist infiltration. Several branches have seemed in danger of being "captured" by persons who appear to adhere more closely to the policy of the Communist Party than to the policies of the National Association of the Advancement of Colored People.[7]

The party's particular approach at a given time depended, of course, on the existing party line. During the late 1920's the Communists aimed at destroying the Association and building separate Negro organizations that would pick up the remains. In the early 1930's that position was slightly altered, but intense efforts to discredit the NAACP continued, and separate party organizations for Negroes were developed. With the United Front line in 1935 came Communist use of

[7] *Ibid.*, pp. 98–99.

the penetration technique against the NAACP, coupled with efforts to develop alliances with it in "front" organizations. An example was the attempt to build a Communist-directed National Negro Congress which would unite a wide range of Negro organizations in a program of political action. During the 1939–1941 period the Communists attacked the NAACP frontally because it would not take an unqualified position in opposition to the defense program. After the German attack on the Soviet Union in June, 1941, the CP did a *volte-face* and with equal vigor and bitterness attacked the Association for not giving unqualified endorsement to the war effort. With the close of World War II and the rapid development of the cold war the whole Communist position underwent another sudden shift. The growing strength of the NAACP, together with growing weaknesses in the Communist ranks, precluded a frontal attack; so the party reverted to the infiltration tactics of an earlier period, especially after 1950, when most of its own race organizations were collapsing. The post-Stalin era has found the CPUSA in an extremely weak position generally and with little prospect for successfully infiltrating or capturing the NAACP or for building its own separate Negro organizations. Here and there it is an irritant to the Association. To the white segregationists it is a godsend, for it provides some slight substance to the charge that racial protest is "Communistic."

In the past there were some members of the NAACP who were also Communists. Quite possibly there are now among the 350,000 members of the Association a handful of individuals whose first allegiance is to the party. Other members of the NAACP, including some of its present national leaders, were at one time somewhat sympathetic toward Marxism and participated in organizations which later proved to be under party control, or at least party influence. There have been Negroes in the NAACP who abandoned it in favor of the

CP or of rival agencies established by the CP. A few NAACP members were the willing, others the unwilling, tools of party functionaries; perhaps a few still are. It should come as no shock that some NAACP branches were captured by Communists; after all, there were hundreds of local branches, whose membership requirements were not too stringent and whose structure was quite loose. It can be assumed that the party has had other influences, difficult to measure, on the NAACP. For example, the CP's involvement in a number of *causes célèbres* in which the Association was also a participant led the latter to fashion tactics that might otherwise not have been developed. The party's emphasis on mass action was a reminder to the NAACP that a broadened membership base was feasible, indeed imperative. Such indirect and frequently negative pressures cannot be treated in detail here; they will be evaluated in the next several chapters.

The few successes must be viewed against the over-all record of Communist failure. Concurrently, the growth of the NAACP must be measured primarily in terms of its cumulative accomplishments, for which the Communists can claim little credit. Time and again the NAACP forced the CP to retreat on its Negro program; more than any other organization, the NAACP presented a bulwark against Communist progress in Negro communities. In sum, the NAACP became a stable, seminal force in American life during the same period that the Communist Party rose and then fell to the point where it can command the loyalties of less than six thousand adherents, among whom only a few are Negroes. How—and, more importantly, why—that development came to pass is the burden of the next five chapters.

II

The First Decade:
1919-1928

DURING its formative years in the United States, the Communist movement consisted of a number of minuscule factions, each of which claimed the only legitimate Marxian ancestry and sole guardianship of the true faith. None of them gave much attention to the Negro question, each apparently assuming that if the race problem arose, it could be readily handled within the faction's general collection of revealed truth. The factions were composed primarily of recent immigrants whose knowledge of the American scene was fragmentary; their familiarity with the colored man and his problems was limited. Speaking English poorly if at all, associating almost exclusively with members of their own ethnic enclaves, the recent arrivals had little or no contact with Negroes—certainly no very meaningful contact.[1] Although some of the factional literature made general reference to the Negro, it did not emphasize the distinctiveness of the group as a racial minority apart from economic class characteristics.

Further, the early Communist cabals were absorbed in bitter, internecine warfare, continuously challenging each other

[1] Theodore Draper, *The Roots of American Communism* (New York: Viking Press, 1957), p. 392.

in order to evoke Soviet approval, which would eventually be bestowed upon one of them. Fighting each other with weapons too brutal for use against the capitalist enemy and employing tactics which extremist movements reserve especially for heretics, the few hundred revolutionary builders of the new society had little time for racial issues.[2] They would be resolved when the true party came to power.

Had the CPUSSR indicated that the Negro question was crucial or that Negro support was essential for a successful Communist revolution in America, the means of securing such support would have become merely one more issue to war about. The different approaches of contending factions would have been magnified out of all proportion, with each group probably compelled, if by nothing more than its own internal dynamics, to dissent violently from all the rest. But the Kremlin gave no sure sign on race until some years later. By that time the Communist movement had been centralized and was undergoing the rapid Stalinization in which settlement of difference by fiat and expulsion tended to become standard.[3]

Another reason for lack of concern for the Negro was the factions' general acceptance of the Marxian doctrine that the real differences among men were economic rather than social, racial, or psychological. Differences of the latter kinds were superficial, and momentary, deriving from more basic economic forces operating over the course of history. Unity of the proletariat was assured by common suffering under capitalist oppressors; as the exploitation increased, workers would come to realize that the enemy was not members of other racial, nationality, and religious groups but capitalists of whatever identity or persuasion. Consequently there was no

[2] James O'Neal and G. A. Werner, *American Communism* (rev. ed.; New York: E. P. Dutton & Co., 1947), p. 114.

[3] Wilson Record, *The Negro and the Communist Party* (Chapel Hill: University of North Carolina Press, 1951), pp. 56–57.

need for special concern about racial minorities, including the Negro, in the building of a party that would challenge and triumph over the dominant economic class. Why develop special strategies and approaches to Negroes or other racial minorities, who would certainly join the struggle in the normal course of events? The early American Communists, without knowing Negroes and without understanding their peculiar status in a biracial order, could declare, along with Debs, that they had nothing special to offer men of color. No more clearly than their Socialist predecessors did Communists then recognize that Negroes perceived the world and the people who wanted to save it through racial eyes.[4]

Even had the Communists been able to end their petty quarrels and had they focused all their energies upon the Negro, they would have met with disappointment, as they were to do later when they did turn to racial issues in the United States. Potential Negro recruits for the new party were few; most Negroes in the urban North, where the party hoped to build its strength, lacked political consciousness and responded only feebly to radical ideologies and movements. Their limited participation in politics was on a short-term, pragmatic basis; like other recent immigrants to the cities, they traded votes for immediate favors and small concessions from local machines. Most politically concerned Negroes were still under the Lincoln spell, bound by habit as well as by meager spoils to the Republican Party. Those bonds were not broken until the advent of Roosevelt and the New Deal.[5]

Although Negroes had entered mass-production plants during World War I, their numbers were not large except in

[4] Sterling D. Spero and Abram L. Harris, *The Black Worker* (New York: Columbia University Press, 1931), p. 314.

[5] There is a substantial literature on the Negro shift from the Republican Party in 1932 and later. Perhaps the best treatment is found in Henry Lee Moon, *Balance of Power: The Negro Vote* (New York: Doubleday and Co., 1948).

packing, coal, steel, and a few other industries. Even there the foothold was precarious, and they suffered disproportionately from layoffs accompanying the peace. Since Negroes were frequently excluded from trade-unions, they were usually beyond the reach of Communists who tried to use existing labor organizations as instruments through which to carry on revolutionary activities. Further, many of the plants employing Negroes were open shops; some of them Negroes had entered as strikebreakers. There was a strong antiunion sentiment among Negroes, rooted in their agrarian backgrounds and the discriminatory practices of the craft organizations. True, Negroes in industry were exploited and used to depress wages; but they could and did find jobs, albeit only the "hot, heavy, and dirty" ones that were least sought by others.[6]

The majority of Negroes were still in the South, working as tenants, sharecroppers, unskilled laborers, and service menials. Isolated from most economic and political movements, they were difficult to reach and cultivate. The task confronting radical organizers was multiplied by the determination of southern whites to perpetuate the Negro's economic bondage and political impotence. Even if some contact had been established, ignorance, apathy, and indifference among the mass of Negroes themselves would have been formidable hurdles. Merely to tackle the obstacles would have required a Herculean effort, a large-scale and well-financed drive to build a following among southern Negroes, who in some states formed close to half the population.[7]

[6] Robert C. Weaver, *Negro Labor* (New York: Harcourt, Brace, 1946), *passim*, and "Negro Labor since 1929," in Arnold Rose, ed., *Race Prejudice and Discrimination* (New York: Knopf, 1953), p. 118.

[7] The Communist Party, in fact, did not contemplate working among southern rural Negroes until after 1928. Then such activity was not only permitted but also dictated by the adoption of the self-determination program by the Sixth World Congress of the Communist International.

Of course, political radicalism among Negroes was not completely unknown. A. Philip Randolph and Chandler Owen, editors of the socialist *Messenger*, tried to spread that secular gospel. They saw the inferiority of the Negro as a product of capitalism and its removal as contingent on reorganization of society along socialist lines. Among Negro intellectuals and trade-unionists Randolph and Owen created something of a stir, but their influence was extremely limited—and has been greatly overdrawn by those historians who all too frequently judge the importance of a political actor primarily by the volume and ready accessibility of his writings.

In New York the New Negro movement was flourishing when the Communists appeared on the scene. Exemplified by Alain Locke, that movement was essentially an artistic and cultural renaissance which touched only a handful of Negroes, primarily the literati, who had few well-articulated political orientations. Moreover, the movement had pronounced overtones of polite Yankee paternalism, in which the whites' central concern was the discovery and enjoyment of creative impulses among Negro writers, artists, and musicians. What was "new" was neither the Negro nor his talents but the white interest and promotion. Racial themes, of course, were not absent from the works of the New Negroes, and, as Lawrence has pointed out, political concerns—equal rights, socialist theories, black nationalism, and separatist ideologies—informed the efforts of some of them.[8] But it would be a mistake to conclude that the disparate and highly individualized challenges represented any specific social movement.

Even among that group of gifted Negroes, who had repudiated traditional race roles and ideas and who might have been considered highly receptive to radical doctrines which would fill the gap, the early Communists made little headway, in part because they did not regard New Negroes as important compared to black industrial workers and in part because

[8] *Op. cit.*, p. 61.

the Communists, as was emphasized earlier, had little understanding of Negro character. A few years later the Communist International (CI) castigated members of the American section for failing to respond more effectively to the New Negro movement by directing it into radical political channels. Further, the CI deplored the absence of concerted effort toward Negro industrial workers. Had the Kremlin been more aware of the difficulties, its criticism might have been less stringent.[9]

As early as 1920 the "Communist Party," a faction dominated by the Russian Federation, which had split from the Socialist Party, took passing cognizance of the Negro question but concluded that "the racial expression of the Negro is simply the expression of his economic bondage and oppression, each intensifying the other." [10] It proposed to do nothing more than carry on agitation among Negro workers to unite them with all class-conscious workers. However, there was no significant follow-up of the declaration with propaganda and organization work by any of the factional contenders. Although they repudiated the Socialist Party generally, the Communists made no departure from the Socialist position on the Negro. If the NAACP was regarded as a significant force in Negro life, there was little indication in the official pronouncements. Nor did the Communists seem to be officially aware that the great bulk of Negroes were in the South and that only a small proportion were industrial laborers.

During the two years following the Bolshevik Revolution, American Communists were confident that the movement would spread to all the developed capitalist nations, including

[9] "Editorial Comment on the 'Negro Question,'" *Communist International*, n.s., no. 8, p. 4.

[10] "Platform of the Communist Party," *American Labor Year Book*, 1920, p. 419.

the United States. Every instance of American labor or political unrest was seen as another battle in the class war. Such conflicts were usually of short duration and had limited results. As revolutionary movements in Europe receded and as the United States moved into a period of "normalcy," American Communists were forced to concede that the capitalist system would not be overthrown immediately. By 1921 the Communist movement in this country could no longer be propelled by sheer revolutionary excitement or vicarious enjoyment of European upheavals. Independent, direct action, which most of the factions advocated in one form or another, had failed, and it was apparent that new strategies were required.[11]

A shift to "boring from within" existing organizations, with emphasis on agitation about more immediate issues, came rather abruptly in the Third World Congress of the Communist International. However, the American Communists in 1921 were still too preoccupied with factional conflicts to give much attention to the recommendations of the CI. Further, the CPUSSR had not yet perfected its organizational dominance in affiliated sections and could not effectively demand that internal rivalries be suppressed. Even in the CPUSSR there were serious factional disturbances that ultimately were to be settled only by exile or the firing squad.[12]

As for the Negro question, the 1921 recommendations of the CI were largely lost. Even had the American splinter groups been united, they would have had only a small apparatus with which to carry out the program. Boring from within existing Negro organizations such as the NAACP was not recommended,

[11] Spero and Harris, *op. cit.*, p. 408.

[12] This matter has been treated so extensively in the literature on both Soviet and American communism that a mere listing of the more important works would occupy a number of pages. What is important is that even prior to the Stalinization of the CPUSSR the activities of American Communists with regard to the Negro question were conditioned by what went on in the Soviet organization.

since the CI held that the only worth-while Negroes were in the trade-unions, or at least in industry. Presumably, non-worker Negro organizations could be by-passed. The combined Negro membership of the factions did not exceed a hundred, and among these were no men of outstanding experience in trade-union work or Negro protest. Later the party fervently courted Negroes who had belonged to the Industrial Workers of the World (IWW), since those Negroes were both racially and politically radical and skilled in industrial organization of black laborers.[13]

The Fourth World Congress of the CI, convening in 1922, provided a more definite clue that Communist work among American Negroes would be intensified. For the first time the matter was brought before the CI officially for a full-dress review. Subsequently a Special Commission on the Negro Question was appointed, one of its main responsibilities being to conduct a thorough investigation and to compile a series of recommendations that could be incorporated in the programs of American Communists. However, there was no indication that strategies used in recruitment of industrial workers could not be applied to Negroes and no adumbration of the later program of Self-Determination in the Black Belt, though some American delegates apparently were impressed by that kind of approach to Russia's minorities.

The Fourth World Congress did emphasize the importance of the American Negro as a revolutionary resource and declared that American Communists had fallen short in not recruiting more colored workers. The same congress anticipated that the Negro question in the United States would be an effective propaganda weapon among colored peoples of the world. Later that possibility was to be more thoroughly exploited, and the idea of using American Negro Communists as

[13] Earl Browder, "A Negro Labor Organizer," *Workers Monthly*, IV (May, 1925), 294.

organizers in Asia and Africa was projected. In 1922, however, it had not yet fully dawned on Communists either in the United States or in the Soviet Union that race discrimination was one of the most vulnerable spots in the capitalist armor.

Reflecting American Communists' lack of appreciation of the Negro question was their failure to build any special organizations among Negroes. No special committees were set up; no front groups were established; no legal defense instruments were developed; no Negro cadres were trained; no attempts to "capture" Negro leaders in nonunion organizations were made. And, of course, no widely publicized campaigns against "white chauvinism" were undertaken within the ranks. That problem had not yet arisen; there were not enough Negroes in the ranks to precipitate the issue.

What was happening to the NAACP during the early 1920's while Communists flayed each other? The NAACP, founded in 1909, had only a few thousand adherents until the war, when conscription of Negroes and new job opportunities for colored workers pushed race issues further into the limelight. With increased mobility and opportunity, Negroes swelled the ranks of the NAACP, especially during 1919, when membership more than doubled, reaching above 91,000. Then came a period of decline. In 1920 there was only a slight drop of about 1,000, and it appeared that the Association might hold most of its wartime gains. However, in 1921 membership plummeted; at the end of the following year not more than 40,000 dues-paying members remained. Some local branches which had flourished during the war folded, and the national headquarters lacked resources with which to revive them. The losses hurt badly since the NAACP depended primarily on dues rather than on philanthropy for financing its work. Those were crisis years, and there was some question of the organization's survival. Internal dissension, however, was not the Association's principal weakness; its main handicap lay in the fact that it was unable to turn a newly developed race consciousness to effective, peacetime account. Like other reformist movements in the postwar period, the Association was the victim of an unfavorable political climate. The national thirst for "normalcy" embraced demands for the *status quo ante* in race relations.

While Negroes had made some wartime gains, even in the South, powerful white southerners were not eager for colored workers and ex-servicemen to take seriously the slogans of democracy and equality which had led black men and women to hope that the American promise would be at least partially fulfilled. Racial protest was equated with "northern" and "foreign-inspired" radicalism in a pattern that was to be repeated a quarter of a century later. Where pressure and persuasion failed to deter protest, southern whites were quick to resort to more time-honored weapons for keeping the Negro in his place. In such circumstances the NAACP, which had always been weak in the South, could not mount an effective offensive.

Negroes who migrated from the South found no utopias in the North. Their economic status was precarious at best; they were among the first to feel the depression of the early 1920's. Unemployment was disproportionately high; underemployment became chronic. Social disorganization, inherent in the uprooting of a rural and quasi-literate people, would have occurred even in favorable economic conditions; depression compounded it. In addition, Negroes met social hostility in the North, frequently at the hands of European immigrants with whom they competed for housing, jobs, public accommodations, and political influence. Negro communities lacked internal social cohesion, with newcomers being looked down on and exploited by some old-timers wise to the ways of city life. Such conditions produced discontent, but of a kind which the NAACP found difficult to channel. Demagogic appeals might have proved effective, at least temporarily, but those were not respectable weapons in the view of Association leaders. Even had the NAACP recruited the Negro migrants, there would have been the problem of making them organization effectives. For that it lacked the resources.

Further handicapping the NAACP were extremist groups operating among both whites and Negroes. Among the former the resurgent Ku Klux Klan made considerable headway. Confined largely to southern and border states in an earlier period, the KKK in the 1920's spread its influence to the North, Midwest, and Southwest. In many localities it employed political means and was thus able to clothe its actions with legality. In some states it became a major force to be reckoned with—for example, in Indiana.[14] One of its chief targets, in addition to Catholics, Jews, and "foreigner," was Negroes—and the NAACP. The latter was subject to virulent attack. Because it had no significant political influence outside a few heavily populated metropolitan centers in the North and its members were disfranchised in the South, the Association was shackled. In contrast to the 1960's, the federal administration in the 1920's showed no disposition to use its executive powers against "hate groups."

As if this were not enough, the NAACP came under attack from another, quite different, quarter. The Garvey Movement, operating within Negro communities primarily through the Universal Negro Improvement Association (UNIA), presented a challenge as forthright as that of the KKK. The relationship between the Garvey Movement and the NAACP merits a long disquisition; a brief summary must suffice here. Marcus Garvey, a Jamaica-born Negro of extremely dark hue, came to the United States during World War I at the invitation of Booker T. Washington, who was interested in some Negro self-help projects which Garvey had launched on his native island. Be-

[14] Robert Moats Miller, "A Note on the Relationship between the Protestant Churches and the Revived Ku Klux Klan," *Journal of Southern History*, XXII (Aug., 1956), 355–368.

fore Garvey arrived Washington died, but this did not deter the Jamaican.

Beginning in New York City, Garvey organized a chapter of the UNIA. Rapidly his influence spread and new locals were set up across the country. Departing from his initial self-help program, Garvey placed more and more emphasis on Negro separatism and black nationalism. Among his proposals was the return of all Negroes to their "African homeland" and establishment of a Negro republic or monarchy with himself as head. Garvey created a number of special organizations to direct the return to a black Canaan. Appealing primarily to the "internal proletariat" among Negroes, he found enthusiastic response from the poor, darker-skinned migrants from the South, to whom the elaborate rituals, colorful regalia, and grandiose titles had a special meaning. Garvey was a showman. Reaching out for an international following, he established his own newspaper and sent emissaries to other countries. He had the common touch, which the more austere—but in the end more realistic—NAACP leaders could never capture.

Increasingly Garvey emphasized racial purity and separatism, rejecting the possibility that members of different races might live in close proximity on an equal basis. Holding a low estimate of lighter-skinned Negroes, he glorified color, insisting that even Jesus Christ was black. He attacked the NAACP and its spokesmen with organizing, writing, and oratorical skills unmatched by any of its other Negro critics. In community after community he challenged its claim to speak for Negroes. Further, he drained off money that might otherwise have gone to the Association. Capitalizing on the disadvantaged position of the darker-hued Negroes, Garvey suggested that the immediate enemy was not the white man but the "tan-skinned," middle-class Negroes who, he said, dominated the NAACP. Following that argument to its logical conclusion, Garvey sought to form cooperative relations with the Klan and the Anglo-

Saxon Clubs in the South. Thus he challenged the NAACP at all levels: ideological, organizational, and personal.

In the columns of *Crisis*, the official NAACP publication, Du Bois carried on a running fight with the Jamaican, trying at first to assess Garvey's program calmly. However, as the UNIA continued to grow and as its attacks on the Association mounted, Du Bois and other NAACP leaders began to deal with him in a less gentlemanly manner. Some NAACP spokesmen were members of the Friends of Negro Freedom, which pressured the United States Department of Justice to bring Garvey to trial on a fraud charge, of which he was subsequently convicted. Sentenced to the Atlanta penitentiary, Garvey served two years and was then paroled and deported. He left few permanent marks, but for a number of years he was a thorn in NAACP's flesh, a reminder of the internal differences of the Negro community and of the Association's own narrow base there.[15] Garvey's present-day counterpart, Elijah Muhammad (Poole) of the Black Muslims, holds a similar view of the NAACP, presents the same kind of challenge, and is willing to make the same kind of alliances, in this case with George Rockwell and the American Nazis.

In spite of these problems, the NAACP's activities during the 1920's were not wholly defensive and unsuccessful. It continued to press for equal justice in the courts. It began a series of legislative moves to outlaw lynching and abolish the poll tax. More able Negroes were drawn into the leadership, and the groundwork for long-range strategies was laid. Through *Crisis* and other publications it tried to heighten interest in the Negro question in the United States and abroad. Only slight attention was paid to left-wing movements, including the Communist, and there is little evidence that the Association was

[15] For a full-scale study of the Garvey Movement, with particular attention to its relations with the NAACP, see Edmund David Cronon, *Black Moses* (Madison: University of Wisconsin Press, 1955).

particularly concerned one way or another with what was happening in the Soviet Union.

From its origins the NAACP was limited by the fact that its leaders did not envision it as a mass organization; the "Talented Tenth" orientation, epitomized—almost caricatured—in the stately and aloof Du Bois, dominated the top staff. The leaders had now experienced some of the problems that plague a rapidly growing social action organization and the even more disturbing difficulties that come with its decline. They were determined to build again, this time on more solid foundations, more slowly. Keenly aware of their limited resources and more realistic than Garvey and his lieutenants about organization matters, they had few illusions about the task confronting them. Such realism, however, had its liabilities in that it restricted their imagination and prevented their recognizing and acting on opportunities that some other organizations among Negroes attempted to grasp.

The response of Negroes to communism in the early 1920's was not one of the problems of the NAACP. The contending Communist factions had little appeal for colored people at any social level, even for intellectuals seeking to link racial concerns to larger issues and ideologies. Further, the Association did not then find itself being ardently wooed by the radical factions, which regarded it as a peripheral force.

Beginning in 1924 the Communists, a bit more unified than in the past, altered slightly their attitudes toward Negroes and toward the NAACP. There were several reasons: immediate proletarian revolution was out of the question; the USSR was seeking internal stability in order to consolidate the revolution and could not lend much support to affiliated sections of the Communist International; the CP in the USSR was still torn by factionalism and by disagreement on the form Communist movements in other countries should take; Communist factions in the United States were under strong attack by the federal government and by the trade-unions. In those circumstances it appeared advisable for the Communists to abandon separatism and direct action and to work through existing organizations. Since appeals to industrial workers had frequently fallen on deaf ears, it was considered expedient to approach other groups, including Negroes, whose grievances might be turned to revolutionary account. In that way the NAACP came under scrutiny.

The Communists' rationale was this: Negroes were the most oppressed group under American capitalism; they should therefore be the most receptive to programs for radical change; Negro industrial workers were the most advanced members of the race and were the logical leaders for a "liberation" drive; however, some Negroes had reaped advantages from the biracial system and would oppose any threat to disrupt the *status quo* in race relations; they occupied important, white-conferred positions, and their efforts to better the Negro's plight required white sanction; among them were the leaders of the NAACP.

Thus the duty of the Communists was to discredit those colored leaders and to develop separate organizations for Negroes. If that proved infeasible, the CP was to bore from within existing race organizations to try to take them away from the black *bourgeoisie*. When developing separate Negro organizations, Communists were to focus on industrial workers and on those few intellectuals who would be sufficiently "advanced" to overcome their social-class identities; that that was not an insuperable task had been demonstrated by Garvey, whom the Communists had fought but who had nevertheless organized Negroes on a mass basis.

The principal drill for boring from within was the Trade Union Educational League (TUEL), which sought to place all eligible Communists in unions vulnerable to penetration; to organize "fractions" within "broad, left-wing, working-class"

37

movements; and to form alliances with dissident elements in labor organizations to capture crucial offices. Particularly were Communists through the TUEL to work on Negro unionists. The Third World Congress of the Red International of Labor Unions instructed the TUEL to pay special attention to the "politically and industrially disfranchised negroes" and to demand that they be given the same social, political, and industrial rights as whites. Further, the TUEL was told to issue a special pamphlet "dealing with negro workers." [16]

The TUEL's greatest headway was made, however, in the needle trades, where unions at that time had only a few Negro (though many foreign-language) members. In the heavy mass-production industries, where most Negro laborers worked, the League made little headway, although it scored some successes in shipbuilding, steel, and coal. In practice the TUEL Negro program was subordinated to the fight for control of union machinery. Further, the Communists themselves were not quite so liberal as they thought on the Negro question. Some TUEL organizers reasoned that since organization of Negroes might lead to support of their right to intermarry with whites, the Negroes were better left unorganized!

Some effort was made to infiltrate the NAACP and the National Urban League (NUL), but the attempts were sporadic, accompanied by frontal propaganda attacks on both organizations. In the face of failure, the Communists resorted to the second tactic, dual organization among Negroes. The Central Committee of the CP authorized formation of the American Negro Labor Congress (ANLC) in early 1925. Negroes from segregated and mixed trade-unions, nonunionized black workers, and selected Negro intellectuals were to be invited to join. Local committees under ANLC direction were to work with black laborers and build a party base among them. The recruits

[16] *Labor Herald: Organ of the Trade Union Educational League*, III (July, 1924), 152.

might then be directed to penetrate existing organizations or to form the nucleus of separate unions.

When the first ANLC convened in Chicago in October, 1925, it was already under acid attack by the American Federation of Labor and by non-Communist Negro trade-unionists, including Philip Randolph, who by then had organized the Brotherhood of Sleeping Car Porters and was trying to bring the Porters into the Federation.[17] Randolph conjectured—rightly, as it turned out—that the ANLC was an abortive move and would only further isolate Negro unionists from the major organizations. However, Du Bois, highly conscious of the Jim Crowism of many AFL affiliates, suggested that the ANLC, together with Randolph's organization of the Porters, was "significant."[18] And Charles S. Johnson in an editorial in *Opportunity*, the Urban League voice, raised pointed questions about the professed AFL solicitude for Negroes who might join the new movement.[19] Neither man, however, endorsed the

Only thirty delegates attended the first meeting of the ANLC; most of them came from local unions under Communist control, and no Negro farmers or sharecroppers were present. The delegates adopted without modification the program proposed earlier by the party Executive Committee. Detailed operating procedures were added, however, with emphasis on concealment of Communist influence and avoidance of aggressive recruitment for the party. Further, delegates recommended ANLC cooperation with "progressive" organizations in the Negro communities, but the term was so restricted as to exclude virtually every group except the CP and the TUEL. Certainly "progressive" did not cover the NAACP.

[17] Brailsford R. Brazeal, *The Brotherhood of Sleeping Car Porters* (New York: Harper & Bros., 1946), 132.

[18] W. E. B. Du Bois, Editorial, *Crisis*, XII (Dec., 1925), 60.

[19] "Labor and Communism," *Opportunity*, III (Dec., 1925).
ANLC.

As Randolph anticipated, the ANLC, although backed by the party and the TUEL, never got off the ground. In 1926 James W. Ford, then a TUEL organizer, attended the annual NAACP conference as a special delegate from the ANLC. Ford submitted a resolution calling for cooperation between the NAACP, the TUEL, and the Brotherhood of Sleeping Car Porters in establishing branches of the ANLC. The resolution was voted down overwhelmingly, an outcome that the ANLC anticipated and for which it probably hoped, since it could then "document" its charge that the NAACP was composed of middle-class Negro "misleaders" with no concern for the colored workingmen, "the only class among Negroes which possesses great universal strength and economic power." [20] The apparent cynicism of the move was not lost on NAACP leaders, and conference delegates received another sharp reminder that the Communists, having entered the race field with some vigor, were prepared to use harsh weapons against those who stood in their way.

Unable to secure the cooperation of such organizations as the NAACP, the ANLC succeeded in establishing only a few local branches during the several years of its existence. Typically they were in centers where the TUEL had some following; indeed, there was considerable duplication in the two memberships. The party hailed the first meeting of the ANLC as a great success and predicted that it would expand rapidly by attracting unorganized Negroes and those Jim Crowed in the AFL. However, the ANLC became even more isolated from Negro industrial workers, not to mention the NAACP, the NUL, and other organizations. The NUL saw the ANLC as a direct threat to its program of establishing new racial employment patterns through negotiations with management. Further, the Negro press, which perceived little good in trade-unionism generally

[20] Robert Dunne, "The NAACP Takes a Step Backward," *Workers Monthly*, V (Aug., 1926), 460.

at the time, periodically castigated the ANLC for its left-wing domination and disruptive tactics. Leading Negro unionists boycotted it and warned their followers to be on guard. Even the party conceded eventually, some five years after the ANLC was founded, that it was a narrow, sectarian organization, isolated from the mass of colored workers, rigid in its tactics, and incapable of cooperation with non-Communist Negro groups.[21]

However, as Brazeal has suggested, there may have been some indirect consequences of ANLC activity, leading to a relaxation in discriminatory policies of the AFL affiliates.[22] Possibly it promoted among Negro workers a less hostile attitude toward organized labor and sparked a few Negro caucuses in mixed unions, but, in the absence of more convincing data, these influences remain conjectural. The historian Charles H. Wesley thought at the time that the organization of the ANLC presaged development of separate Negro unions and mirrored the potential militancy of colored workers.[23] He was wrong.

Although the ANLC was never considered much of a threat by the NAACP, another Communist-controlled organization established during the same year was viewed in a quite different light, for the International Labor Defense (ILD) proposed to invade a field that the Association had come to regard more or less as its exclusive domain. One of a number of organizations established by the Communist International to exploit court cases for revolutionary propaganda, the ILD was affiliated with the Red International of Class War Prisoners Aid. The ILD gave as reasons for its formation "the encroachment of local agencies upon the constitutional rights and civil liberties,

[21] James W. Ford, *The Negro and the Democratic Front* (New York: International Publishers, 1938), 81–83.

[22] *Op. cit.*, pp. 132–133.

[23] *Negro Labor in the United States* (New York: Viking Press, 1927), p. 279.

the activities of extra-legal organizations . . . in restricting the freedom of activity of people because of race, nationality, creed, color, or class." [24]

The ILD soon indicated that it would be concerned to a large extent with cases involving Negroes, and named William L. Patterson, a Negro lawyer and journalist, to the post of executive secretary. Patterson had visited the Soviet Union in the early 1920's, attended special party training schools in Moscow, and returned to the United States with great enthusiasm for the new workers' fatherland. Whether Patterson was formally a member of the CP at that time or later, he adhered closely to the Communist position on every issue during the entire career of the ILD. After surveying the fifteen-year history of the ILD prior to 1940, Ralph Bunche pointed out that all actions of the organization reflected "the national interest of the Soviet Union" and that its concern with the American Negro was "purely a tactical one dictated by political expediency." [25]

The Communists had pressing reasons for organizing the ILD: since 1910 the NAACP had come to be recognized as the voice of Negroes seeking justice through the courts. Although the Association had lost strength during the early 1920's, it was by no means dead, and it was still the organization to which Negroes turned in their struggles for fair trials and the minimal conditions of citizenship. As long as the NAACP fought effectively on immediate, dramatic cases readily understood by the average Negro, who could easily identify with the victims, the Communists were less likely to attract a large colored following. Hence it was necessary for the ILD not only to

[24] Ralph Bunche, "Programs, Ideologies, Tactics and Achievements of Negro Betterment and Interracial Organizations" (MS prepared as part of preliminary research for Gunnar Myrdal's *An American Dilemma;* now in Schomburg collection, New York Public Library), p. 708.

[25] *Ibid.,* p. 695.

concern itself with racial injustice in the courts but also to attack the NAACP's legal efforts, attempting to discredit it in the colored community. To that end the ILD, through the *Worker, Communist, New Masses,* and other party publications, carried on a campaign of vilification.

The Association was first branded as an organization controlled by white philanthropists and completely subservient to white capitalists in the Republican Party.[26] Later it was castigated for being an instrument of "Negro bourgeois reformers" who repudiated the technique of "mass pressure" on the courts and deliberately concealed the class character of law and justice in a capitalist society.[27] Clashes between the ILD and the NAACP became more frequent, reaching a climax when the CP and the ILD moved in on the famed Scottsboro cases in the early 1930's. No other event more clearly revealed the basic differences between the Communist Party and the NAACP than did this *cause célèbre* in which the Association tried to save the lives of nine colored boys and the party tried to win converts to communism. In the next chapter the Scottsboro case will receive detailed attention.

During the middle and late 1920's the NAACP would have fought the Communists more vigorously had it regarded them as a serious threat and had it not been preoccupied, as in the earlier part of the decade, with its own internal weaknesses and attacks from other outsiders, as well as with heavier responsibilities in fighting for the objectives for which it was founded. As an action organization the NAACP was handicapped, almost fatally, by inadequate funds, a limited field staff, unstable local branches, a lack of allies, and a clumsy, ineffective administrative apparatus. However, it did make its influence felt in many

[26] Robert Minor, "The First Negro Workers Congress," *Workers Monthly,* V, 73.

[27] Editorial, "Betrayal by the NAACP," *New Masses,* XIV (Jan. 8, 1935), 6.

ways; for instance, by publicizing the American Negro's plight, primarily through *Crisis*, which remained under Du Bois' editorship.

Circulation of the little protest magazine did not fluctuate alarmingly during that time, though there was a drop from 37,000 in 1923 to 30,000 in 1928. Having a relatively free hand, Du Bois pushed provocative ideas toward both Negroes and whites. Some proposals did not rest well with the more conservative members of the NAACP Executive Board, and there were grumblings about the fierce independence and aloofness of the editor. Although he had only limited affiliations with international social or racial movements, Du Bois sought continuously to link NAACP activities with larger ideologies, particularly Pan-Africanism. Moreover, at least by implication, he was critical of what he thought was the too narrow, legalistic approach to race questions by the Association. *Crisis* became a journal of opinion and ideas; thoughtful men could engage in dialogues about problems of the race and what ought to be done about them. Looking through the racial literature of the era, one comes upon *Crisis* as upon a bright star in a generally murky sky.

Membership in the NAACP continued to drop throughout the entire period. Whereas in 1923 the Association could boast of 14,000 additional members over the previous year, in 1928 it could claim a *total* of only 23,500. The losses hurt not only because they cut down the number of organization effectives in local communities but also because they drastically reduced funds available to the national office. In order to finance the famed Sweet case in Detroit (which will be discussed shortly) the NAACP had to make special appeals to affluent Negroes and white sympathizers. The same was true in the Nixon case, which challenged the white primary in El Paso, Texas. The NAACP's investigation of the shocking treatment of Negroes in the Mississippi flood-relief program of 1927 could not have been conducted on funds from regular sources. The Sweet case alone cost the Association $37,000, only a small portion of which was available in the national treasury at the time.[28] One of the liabilities of financing activities by special drives was the fact that Negroes developed the habit of waiting for crises to develop rather than supporting their protest organizations through regular financial contributions and active participation. Although necessary in the circumstances, hat-in-handism was scarcely the way to build a sturdy, confident movement that American Negroes could call their own; to that extent an earlier Communist criticism had some substance.

The losses of members and funds were not due to inroads made by the Communists. The party did appeal to a few Negro intellectuals of the type that could be found in the NAACP and in the Friends of Negro Freedom. But from the small number of Negroes joining the CP, the ANLC, and the ILD it is clear that the Communists obtained few such recruits from any source, even during the late years of the decade when their "Negro work" was greatly intensified. The reversals and tribulations of the NAACP during that period had a number of historical antecedents. There had been, for example, the decline of Negro organizations during the post-Reconstruction period, a phenomenon thoroughly explored by Rayford W. Logan in *The Negro in American Life and Thought*.[29]

With the Association's members and funds leaking away, its leaders began as early as 1924 to cast about for allies; one place they looked was in the "Negro Sanhedrin" which convened at Chicago in February of that year. Initiated primarily by Kelly Miller, a professor at Howard University, that gathering of black elders included representatives of fraternal, welfare,

[28] The account of these several activities of the NAACP during this period is based primarily on Walter White, *How Far the Promised Land* (New York: Viking Press, 1956).

[29] New York: Harper & Bros., 1954.

religious, and protest organizations. Spokesmen of radical and
trade-union groups were not invited. Some of these established
guardians of the race were disturbed about the declared intentions of the Communists to snare Negro innocents, but their
chief concern was Garvey's UNIA, which was then reaching
its apex. To meet neither of the threats, however, did they
propose mass organization of lower-strata black folk.

Most of the Sanhedrin delegates came from and accepted
the philosophy of the "Talented Tenth," expounded earlier by
Du Bois. Holding that the struggle for racial rights was primarily the responsibility of the gifted Negro, they proposed to
place their prestige and influence on the line to wring from the
white powers concessions that in the end would benefit less
happily endowed members of the race. The movement they
conceived was *for* the people, not *of* the people. Although all
the participants admittedly were talented, some groups believed themselves patently more talented than others; that fact
led to so much jockeying and maneuvering that no agreement
could be reached on a joint course of action.

The elders knew what they were against—the Communists,
Garvey, the Ku Klux Klan, the Anglo-Saxon Clubs, lynching,
disfranchisement, and racial injustice generally; they could not
agree on what they were for or how to get it. The NAACP leaders went to the Sanhedrin hoping to be draped with the mantle
of race leadership. They returned home bare-shouldered, disappointed, bitter—yet no less determined to carry on than had
been their predecessors.

The Communists disdained the Sanhedrin gathering, though
they did castigate Miller and the other participants for their
Talented Tenth outlook and for barring members of extremist
and labor organizations. The Sanhedrin's failure reinforced the
Communists' conviction that Negro middle-class organizations
would not—in fact, could not—wage an effective fight for race
rights. There was no gloom in Communist circles when the

Sanhedrin collapsed, but there could have been little joy in the fact that none of the delegates walked from the final session to the party's Chicago headquarters to ask for a sign-up card.

In spite of its weakened condition and its failure to gain strength through forming alliances, the NAACP, during the second half of the "normalcy" decade, did engage successfully in some crucial battles. It emerged, if not a final victor, at least a tactical winner. In a number of court cases the Association began systematic constitutional challenges to institutionalized instruments of racial exclusion. Additionally it intervened in a number of trials in which gross injustices to Negroes had already been perpetrated or obviously would occur if it did not intercede.

Perhaps the most important case in the latter category was that of Dr. Osian Sweet and his family in Detroit. In September, 1925, the Sweets moved into a home purchased in a middle-class white neighborhood. On the first night of occupancy, September 8, a white mob gathered outside the house and threw stones. Although the police were summoned by Dr. Sweet, a licensed physician, they refused to provide protection; some officers even mingled with and encouraged members of the crowd. On the following night, when an even larger mob assembled, two Negro men passing by from work were severely beaten by whites. Dr. Sweet then turned off the house lights, fearing that the mob would break in, whereupon shots were fired into the house through the doors and windows. The Sweets fired back, killing a white man who had been in the forefront of the screaming attackers.

The police then appeared in force for the first time and arrested, not the rioters who had fired on the Sweet home, but all members of the Sweet household, each of whom was charged with murder. The NAACP investigated and agreed to handle the defense, retaining Clarence Darrow as chief counsel.

The first trial, before Judge Frank Murphy of the Recorder's Court, resulted in a hung jury, which might have reached a verdict of guilty had Darrow not scaled new heights of eloquence in his summary. In the second trial the defendants were tried separately, and Henry Sweet, a son, against whom the prosecution thought it had the strongest case, was tried first. He was acquitted, and cases against the other defendants were dropped. Great publicity in the Negro press emphasized the crucial role played by the NAACP in the Sweets' defense. However, neither that nor other incidents evoking favorable reaction in Negro communities led many dues-paying recruits to Association headquarters. The Communists raised some propaganda noise about the Sweet case, but they could scarcely attack the NAACP except to assert that, although it might win a tactical victory in the courts and save the lives of the Sweet family, it was by its very nature incapable of extending the fight for racial rights to the great mass of Negroes.

In the *Nixon* vs. *Herndon* case the NAACP achieved one of its first victories in the long battle to outlaw the white primary. In 1927 Dr. L. A. Nixon, with the aid of the Association, challenged a Texas statute adopted following enactment of the Seventeenth Amendment, which provided for direct election of United States senators. The law declared that no Negro would be eligible to participate in a Democratic Party election in Texas. Because Dr. Nixon was colored, he was refused a ballot, whereupon he filed a damage suit against El Paso election officials. In the lower courts the case was dismissed. On appeal to the United States Supreme Court, however, the dismissal was overruled in a majority decision written by Mr. Justice Holmes, and the Texas statute was declared unconstitutional.

The NAACP thought that at long last it had won reenfranchisement of Negroes in the South, but it soon discovered that white Democrats were prepared to use every legal—or frequently illegal—stratagem for preventing Negroes from obtaining citizenship rights. Dan Moody, the Texas governor, immediately called a special session of the legislature to pass laws empowering the Democratic Party in Texas to make its own rules concerning those eligible to participate in primaries. (Other states followed Texas' lead, and a long struggle in the courts was necessary before the NAACP finally overturned the white primary.) Thus the NAACP's legal victory in the Nixon case was soon nullified, and the organization's critics, particularly the Communists, used that fact to proclaim again the futility of legalistic approaches in securing racial political rights in capitalist America.

During the same year the NAACP intervened in behalf of the Negro victims of the Mississippi flood, who also became victims of white planters and relief administrators. Upon receiving reports that Negro refugees were suffering salient discrimination, the Association sent Walter White to investigate. He found the reports to be an understatement. Some Negroes were penned in what amounted to concentration camps; National Guardsmen were ordered not to release them except in the custody of their landlords. In many cases Negroes were forced to pay for relief supplies which had been given free to the distributors by the American Red Cross. When they were unable to pay, the money was put up by plantation owners and other employers, to whom the Negroes were thereupon in debt for "furnish." Under armed guard the Negroes were then taken to plantations or sawmills to work off their obligations.

White's sensational exposé created quite a stir, not only among Negroes but in the white community as well. Herbert Hoover, whose reputation as a relief administrator was substantial, denied the allegations. He did, however, appoint an investigating committee headed by Dr. Robert R. Moton, president of Tuskegee Institute. Much to Hoover's chagrin, the report of the Moton group confirmed rather than refuted

49

White's findings. Even so, remedial action was slow, and many weeks passed before the worst abuses of the colored flood refugees were ended. Hoover's handling of the Mississippi flood disaster embittered many Negroes and without doubt contributed to their disillusionment with the Republican Party, although their traditional loyalty was not seriously breached until the depression and the rise of Franklin D. Roosevelt to leadership of the Democrats.

The flood disaster had a special significance for the NAACP. It demonstrated the effectiveness of an aroused body of public opinion in getting action from agencies of the federal government to obtain more equitable treatment for Negroes under existing law. The technique was to be used and sharpened increasingly during the depression years. Before the coming of the New Deal, Negro leaders were thus already sensitized to the possibilities of federal administrative action in the area of race rights, and they moved to organize and exert pressures through such *ad hoc* groups as the Joint Committee on National Recovery as well as through the established race organizations. The efforts culminated in Roosevelt's issuance, in June, 1941, of Executive Order 8802, which banned racial discrimination in war production industries. Roosevelt was the first president to use executive powers to ameliorate discrimination. As the strategic value of the Negro vote has grown, the White House has bestirred itself more energetically in behalf of colored citizens. President Kennedy has brought executive initiative to a high peak in his campaign to win franchisement for Negroes in the rural South. But discussion of these events is premature here.

During the 1920's white mob violence came to be looked upon with growing distaste, even in the South; lynching was not so prevalent as it had been; the white primary was challenged for the first time; and on at least one occasion the federal administration was forced to intervene in behalf of Negroes below the Mason-Dixon line. Despite the fact that the NAACP had been conspicuously responsible for much of the progress, it ended the decade with fewer members than it had at the beginning. But if the Association could claim few organizational gains, the Communists had even less to boast about. Total membership in the party in 1928, according to official spokesmen who characteristically exaggerated the numbers, was 14,000, only 9,300 of which were actual dues payers. Although membership was claimed to have risen 1,000 a year since 1925, the Communists barely recouped their losses of the early twenties. The party itself estimated that only 200 Negroes had joined the ranks, although it was claimed that 300 more had recently made application as a result of an organizational drive. With so small a total membership, less than 2 per cent of it Negro, the party was obviously something less than representative of the mass of toilers, black or white, for whom it claimed to speak.

III

The Depression Era: 1929-1935

A NEW era in relations between the NAACP and the CPUSA was introduced in the late 1920's and early 1930's. It was precipitated by two developments: (1) a drastic shift in the Communist Party's program in general and on the Negro question in particular, growing out of directives from the Sixth World Congress of the Communist International in 1928, and (2) the onset of the great American depression, whose impact was felt particularly by Negroes, most of whom were in marginal economic positions. The changes in the Communist Party program had wide implications for its approach to and work among Negroes, fostering a militancy which the NAACP could not take lightly. On the other hand, the depression, initially at any rate, confused and weakened the NAACP and precipitated problems, organizational and programmatic, with which it was poorly equipped to deal. Since an understanding of these two novel elements in the American racial scene is essential to a grasp of the detailed relations of the CP and the Association during the interval from 1929 to 1935, it might be well to examine the elements in some detail.

The new Communist Party line abandoned the "boring from within" tactics of the preceding period. Why? First, the evidence was impressive that the previous approach was a failure, the attempts to penetrate trade-unions, left-of-center parties, and racial and ethnic groups having produced few concrete results. Although the efforts had not been uniformly unrewarding, they had fallen so far short of the mark that leaders of the Communist International were convinced that only a complete reorientation of the CP strategy in the United States would do. Second, the serious internal crises in the Soviet Union had abated somewhat by the late 1920's, and the Communist International leaders, now subservient to Stalin, believed that a more vigorous assault on capitalist systems, including that in the United States, should be launched.

At its core the new strategy entailed development of separatist organizations dedicated to an independent, uncompromising assault on capitalism, not only by fomenting proletarian revolutions in the more highly developed countries but also by fostering "national liberation" movements in colonial areas. Anticolonial activity would be an indirect way of attacking the major industrial powers. The new strategy, originating in the Kremlin and imposed on the affiliated sections of the Communist International over the doubts of some and the opposition of others, was to become the operating code of the CP in the United States.[1] What were its specific implications for American Negroes?

Generally, the new program required development of revolutionary, dual organizations in all areas of CP activity. The targets included industrial workers, intellectuals, sharecroppers, tenants, nationality groups, Negroes, and such other potentially dissident elements as might be brought, for whatever reasons, under Communist influence. The old in-boring apparatus was dismantled; instead of trying to capture indigenous protest groups from within, the party began a program to try to drain off members from those groups to swell the ranks of the new party organizations. To that end, unsympathetic lead-

[1] Jay Lovestone, "The Sixth World Congress of the Communist International," *Communist*, VII (Nov., 1928), 659–675.

ers of indigenous groups were to be subjected to continuous, merciless attack which would brand them as "social fascists," "misleaders of labor," and "betrayers of the Negro people." [2]

Revolutionary trade-unions were to be organized through the Trade Union Unity League (TUUL), which quickly supplanted the Trade Union Educational League. Radically inclined members of the Socialist Party and unhappy members of other left-wing political movements were to be enticed directly into the Communist Party. In the Midwest and South separate revolutionary organizations of farmers, tenants, and sharecroppers were to be built on a program of land confiscation and redistribution and posed against older agrarian organizations such as the Grange. For Negroes there would be new agencies arrayed against the NAACP and the Urban League. If possible, revolutionary organizations of artists and writers were to be established with a view to using their talents for propaganda work. [3]

Specific organizations which eventually emerged were, in addition to the TUEL for industrial workers, the Sharecroppers Union for southern farm laborers and tenants, the American Student Federation for the left-wing college crowd, the League of Struggle for Negro Rights (LSNR) for colored people, and the League Against War and Fascism to accommodate a wide range of people sympathetic to Soviet foreign policy. Some of the new organizations got under way only slowly and might have died a-borning except for the worsening depression, which fostered radical upsurges that Communists were to some extent able to capitalize.

The party developed a systematic analysis of the American Negro question for the first time. A new program, "Self-

[2] William Z. Foster, "The Decline of the American Federation of Labor," *Communist*, VIII (Jan., 1929), *passim*.

[3] Eugene Gordon, "Negro Novelists and the Negro Masses," *New Masses*, VIII (July, 1933), 16.

Determination for Negroes in the Black Belt," was adopted by the Communist International over the skepticism of American Communists, who, having made little headway among Negroes in the previous period, were in no position to say "no" effectively. The Communist International had long been aware of the American Negro's indifference to the CPUSA. It was also aware that the only mass movement ever organized among American black folk was Marcus Garvey's UNIA. And what did Garvey stress? Racial separation.

Prior to the 1928 meeting of the CI, its Executive Committee circulated a series of "theses" on the Negro question in the United States. They declared that Negroes in this country constituted a nation and that their exploitation was part and parcel of the same capitalist imperialism which crushed other colored peoples under foot in Asia and Africa. Therefore, it was argued, a solution of the Negro problem in the United States could be found in the doctrines on minorities, imperialism, and nationalism developed by Lenin and presumably applied by the USSR in dealing with Russian racial and cultural minorities.

Negroes in the United States were deemed by the party to meet every criterion of nationhood. They were a distinctive racial and cultural group—an "historically evolved, stable entity, defined by language, territory, economic life and psychological make-up manifested in a community of culture," a definition suggested by Stalin, presumably drawn from Lenin's works on nationalism. If American Negroes were a nation, they should be approached on the same basis that Communists had approached oppressed, racially homogeneous, colonial peoples elsewhere. Moreover, it logically followed that American Negroes had the same right to self-determination, which would presumably lead to the establishment of an independent Negro republic in the area of "black majority" in the South. The significance of the new line of thought can scarcely be overstated, for it was to become the guiding theory of CP work among American Negroes.[4]

The proposal was adopted by the Sixth World Congress in spite of misgivings among the American delegates for reasons similar to those earlier voiced by British Communists.[5] The two English-speaking delegations thought the approach unrealistic. Nonetheless, the American Communists went along with the "majority," substituting Stalin's theoretical brilliance about nations in general for their own judgment about a situation they knew specifically. One American delegate even thanked the CI later for exercising its supreme intelligence over those not privy to the inner truths of Marxism-Leninism.[6]

To implement the self-determination doctrine American Communists were directed to take a number of specific steps: link all short-term demands in behalf of Negroes with the ultimate goal, bring "wide masses of Negroes" into struggle alongside the CP, select issues that could be joined readily with the self-determination struggle, place Communists in the forefront of the Negro liberation movement, develop a revolutionary trade-union movement among Negroes and whites in the South while recruiting the "more advanced elements" for the party, "expose" bourgeois Negro leaders who rejected self-determination for the race, and coordinate the struggle for Negro rights in the North with the separate-nation move in the South.

Here, obviously, was a big order whose filling was not helped by the confusion in American Communist ranks that followed its adoption. Much soul-searching took place in the party journals; the nub of it is aptly summarized in the words

[4] James S. Allen, *The Negro Question in the United States* (New York: International Publishers, 1936), *passim*.

[5] A. Shiek, "The Comintern Program and the Racial Problem," *Communist International*, V (Aug. 15, 1928), 407.

[6] Lovestone, *loc. cit.*

56

of one writer: "I know that self-determination is correct for else it would not have been approved by the Communist International. However, I have difficulty understanding it, and I would like our more advanced comrades to help me." Even more dismayed were the few Negro Communists themselves, whose subsequent effectiveness seemed to vary inversely with the vigor of their allegiance to the self-determination line. Jacob Spolansky has described the dilemma of William Nowell, who for a number of years was a leading Negro Communist in the Detroit area, in trying to digest and propagate the "Made in Moscow" version of the Negro American's destiny.[7] For many Negroes, the proposal of a separate nation sounded like a red-winged Jim Crow.

For the first time Communists became active among southern Negroes.[8] Their efforts were directed along several lines and aimed principally at organizing branches of the party itself, revolutionary unions in steel, coal, and textiles through the TUUL, revolutionary associations of tenants and share-croppers, and protest councils among the unemployed. Outside the South the Communists tried to organize revolutionary unions and affiliate them with the TUUL, local councils of the unemployed, and, for Negroes specifically, the League of Struggle for Negro Rights. In the South as well as in the North attempts were made to establish the organizations on an interracial basis. Action on the immediate needs of each group was urged, but always with the understanding that it must contribute to the larger revolutionary goals.[9]

To carry its program of revolutionary unionism to Negro

[7] *The Communist Trail in America* (New York: Macmillan Co., 1951), pp. 33–39.

[8] House Committee on Un-American Activities, *The American Negro in the Communist Party*, report, 83rd Cong., released by the Committee Dec. 22, 1945, pp. 4–5. Cited hereafter as *Amer. Negro in CP*.

[9] Stuart Jamieson, *Labor Unionism in American Agriculture* (Washington: Bureau of Labor Statistics, 1945), chap. vii.

57

workers, the TUUL established special shop committees. James W. Ford, a Negro associated with the old TUEL, was named special organizer to assist other TUUL functionaries in recruiting Negro industrial workers. Among the TUUL affiliates were the National Miners Union, Needle Trades Workers Industrial Union, National Textile Workers Union, Metal Trades Industrial Union, Marine Workers League, and later, the Sugar Beet Workers Union, Building Trades Industrial League, Auto Workers Union, Printing and Publishers Industrial League, Railroad Amalgamation Committee, and the Food and Packinghouse Workers Industrial Union.

Although in some of the industries—steel, coal, and meat packing—in which the TUUL operated there were substantial numbers of Negroes, it obtained few colored recruits and even failed to secure an impressive white following; total strength of the TUUL never exceeded 100,000, despite considerable unrest among workers in the throes of depression. The proportion of Negroes is not definitely known, but probably not more than 5 per cent of its total strength was Negro. Communist activity among Negro industrial workers and the unemployed touched only a few NAACP members directly, since they were drawn primarily from the Negro middle class and were not so adversely affected economically as those in the lower strata. However, Association leaders were increasingly disturbed by the plight of the less fortunately situated groups, realizing that with intensification of the depression those people might become more responsive to extremist appeals.

With unemployment mounting, with Negroes unable to find jobs, and with those on relief proportionately twice as numerous as in the general population, the NAACP leaders knew the old methods had to be reviewed. They publicized the growing poverty and degradation of Negro communities. They encouraged organization of the black workers and the unemployed. Although they had reservations about the auspices under which such collective action took place, they were loath to counsel against the action, especially since they themselves could not come up with a workable alternative. The National Urban League took a similar position, even sponsoring workers' study groups in an effort to train Negroes for union participation. Even so, during the early depression years the NAACP and the NUL were more spectators than participants in the struggle to organize Negro workers into trade-unions.

Therefore the most forthright clashes between the NAACP and the Communists came in other spheres, specifically when the Association confronted the League of Struggle for Negro Rights and the International Labor Defense. The LSNR was organized in November, 1930, for the purpose of aligning a broad cross section of Negro groups behind a comprehensive race program under the firm control of the Communist Party.[10] Although a number of non-Communists held office in the League, there was never any doubt about where the power, such as it was, lay. The broad and ambitious League program was directed, as was that of the later National Negro Congress, toward Negro women, sharecroppers, workers, businessmen, soldiers, and students. In other words, in line with the self-determination theory, it proposed to cut across class lines.

The League did not have something for everybody; to the NAACP, for example, it offered no comfort. In an official declaration the League said it would have no truck with the leaders of the Association who "aped" their ideal, Booker T. Washington, in bowing and scraping in "the ante-rooms of the mighty." [11] Specifically it attacked W. E. B. Du Bois, William Pickens, and Walter White. Such charges had to be answered. The method the Association leaders employed was to stress

[10] LSNR, *Equality, Land and Freedom: A Program for Negro Liberation* (New York: LSNR 1933)

[11] *Ibid.*, pp. 12–13.

the basic differences between the NAACP and the Communists
and to expose the Communist affiliations of most of the League
officers, sharpening its indictment by pointing out that the
League had accepted without question the whole self-
determination-for-Negroes program that originated in the
party.

Although the League was committed to obtaining a broad
Negro following, it quickly alienated itself from the institution in which most Negroes were to be found—the church.
Proclaiming its acceptance of Marxist materialism, identifying
religion with ignorance and superstition, and branding colored
ministers and their followers as, at best, victims of unfortunate
historical circumstance and, at worst, "lickspittles" of their
white masters, the League cut itself off from black men and
women who had found their main solace in the pews of rural
churches. Even the more sophisticated city dwellers were of-
fended by the party's rude rejection of the Negro's faith. For
most Negroes the gospel according to Matthew continued to
have more appeal than the gospel according to Marx.

In contrast, the NAACP had long recognized that religion was
too deeply engrained in American Negro life to be discarded
as an instrument for rallying Negroes against oppressive racial
practices. Indeed, both leaders and members of the NAACP
were usually men of rather firm religious commitments; for
them an acceptance of the League's position would have meant
not only organizational disaster but personal apostasy as well.
The local minister was often the local Association president
and attempted to persuade his flock that, far from being at
cross-purposes, the NAACP and the Christian church were striving for the same goals.

Both the NAACP and the League were compelled to involve
themselves in the immediate economic and social problems of
Negroes. Both were handicapped by the fact that the problems were of such magnitude that no private efforts could deal

with them adequately; the situation called for a concerted national attack, which was eventually undertaken by the New Deal. At the end of its short career the League could point to no significant contribution on any of the specific, immediate issues with which Negroes were concerned: employment, voting, education, housing, and civil rights. As the party itself was later to admit, the League, in addition to the major handicap indicated above, was hobbled by a narrow, sectarian ideological image. Even Negro intellectuals, who might have been expected to be impressed by its radical ideology and ambitious program, were, with very few exceptions, unresponsive. Although the NAACP took cognizance of the League's existence and issued periodic blasts against it, the portion of its energies expended on the League was small; they were needed elsewhere, and the threat posed by the League seemed mild compared to the threat posed by the depression. During the 1929–1935 period the NAACP gained few recruits; the League fared even more poorly, despite energetic moves to enlist Negro nationalists who had earlier responded to Garvey.

The International Labor Defense, however, was another story. From it came the most effective Communist challenge to the NAACP during the 1929 to 1935 period. The central purpose of the ILD was to use the courts not for the usual juridical purposes but as a means of criticizing capitalist justice and spreading Communist propaganda.[12] Its technique was to intervene in trials in which members of Communist organizations or of some group to which it wanted to make a special appeal were defendants. It would then proceed to make financial, organizational, and propaganda hay out of such trials by appealing for defense funds, organizing special committees, and widely publicizing the issues to ILD and Communist Party advantage. There was no way to lose—if a case was decided against it, the ILD could charge injustice by class courts; if the decision

[12] Bunche, *op. cit.*, p. 695.

was favorable, it could emphasize the power of mass pressure exerted through Communist leadership.

From the time of its formation until the early 1930's the ILD, although handling some Negro cases, had not found one which deeply stirred the colored community. Furthermore, not one of the cases that did attract attention had been in the South. The Scottsboro case, which emerged from rural Alabama in 1931, was a godsend.[13] Nine Negro youths, some of them mere boys, were accused of raping two white girls while traveling in an open freight car through northern Alabama. Although the girls were of bad repute and gave testimony which did not hang together, a local court overrode the boys' protestations of innocence, found them guilty, and sentenced eight of them to death. The long legal struggle that followed dramatized more than any other experience of that period the inherent differences between the NAACP and the ILD; moreover, it brought into major battle two organizations and ideologies which theretofore had merely skirmished.

When it entered the Scottsboro case, the NAACP knew it would be bucking the white reactionaries of the South; it did not anticipate that on that particular issue it would be fighting the Communists as well or that so long a struggle would ensue.[14] The NAACP was disconcerted not only by the violence of southern reaction to the alleged rape of two loose white girls by nine Negro boys but also by the swiftness and the resourcefulness with which the party moved into the case.

The Association's remaining faith in "responsible" southern judges and other "decent" white elements in the South was shaken to its very roots when the most crucial of all tests was applied. The confidence of its leaders in themselves, the organization, and its techniques was, if not shattered, weakened at

[13] Harry Haywood, "The Scottsboro Decision," *Communist*, XI (Dec., 1932), 1075.

[14] White, *Promised Land*, p. 214.

many points. At the same time there appeared on the scene a rival organization which, for the moment at least, appeared more able to challenge the prejudiced white newspapers, bigoted judges, demagogic prosecutors, and tobacco-chewing, near-hysterical jurors. All had to be overcome if the Negro youngsters were to obtain fair trials. Deserted by most of its white Southern friends and sympathizers, criticized even by some of its own moderate Negro supporters for its ineffectual action, under attack from the left, and in the throes of an internal crisis, with resources at a low ebb, the NAACP occupied a precarious position.

For the party, on the other hand, Scottsboro was an opportunity of the first magnitude. For the first time the ILD had an issue on which it could make an effective bid for Negro attention; the case was loaded with propaganda possibilities, the like of which not even the most imaginative party devotee could have foreseen. Here was a chance not only to carry its message to the Negro masses but also to link racial injustice to the very foundations of the bourgeois order. Finally, the Scottsboro case provided grist for the world-wide propaganda mill of the Comintern, which was committed to undermining the capitalist hold on colored peoples.

Few Negroes could understand the finer points of Marx's materialism, grasp the meaning of Lenin's theory of imperialism, or fathom the intent of the self-determination doctrine. They did know, either directly or indirectly, the face of southern white justice. No one needed to draw them a picture of the consequences for an accused Negro when an Alabama white woman, however unsavory of background or for whatever motives, yelled "rape." What black man did not identify to some degree with the accused Scottsboro boys?

When the nine Negroes were indicted, convicted, and with one exception given the death penalty—all within a period of less than three weeks—the NAACP intervened and attempted to handle the defense against obviously overwhelming odds. The ILD prejudiced the case still further by sending the presiding judge a telegram in which it threatened that he would be held "personally responsible" unless the defendants were released immediately.[15] It is now apparent, although it might not have been to some people at the time, that the ILD was more concerned with the propaganda aspects of the trials than with the guilt or innocence, the conviction or acquittal of the nine defendants. A quick acquittal would have disarmed the Communists; a quick conviction and execution would have demonstrated the ILD's ineffectiveness. But a case that would drag on and on through the courts was made to order for the comrades.

Having lost the first round, the NAACP moved to appeal the convictions to higher courts, sticking to strict legal procedures. In the interim, however, the ILD, spotting the propaganda gold glistening there for the taking, approached the parents of the condemned youths and persuaded some of them to entrust further handling of the cases to the ILD itself. ILD representatives told the parents that the NAACP was planning to desert the boys and possibly would have them plead guilty in exchange for promises of life imprisonment. Knowing little about the NAACP or the CP and convinced of the innocence of their offspring, some parents were relieved to accept ILD help.[16] Simultaneously the CP, the ILD, the LSNR, and the TUUL loosed an all-out propaganda campaign against the Association and its leaders. Having discredited the NAACP in the eyes of some Negroes because it refused to denounce the whole judicial system, the ILD set about to make Scottsboro not only an American but a world *cause célèbre*. With the aid of Communist-affiliated organizations over the globe it was able to accomplish its objectives.

[15] Walter White, *A Man Called White* (New York: Viking Press, 1949), 128.
[16] Quentin Reynolds, *Courtroom* (New York: Popular Library, 1957), p. 244.

In those circumstances the NAACP, whose orderly, juridical approach had been frustrated by the ILD, withdrew from the Scottsboro defense. Realizing that it would then have to demonstrate concrete results acceptable to Negroes by doing something more than stirring up a propaganda fuss, the ILD retained the famed criminal lawyer, Samuel Liebowitz, to handle the case (the singular form is used though technically the charges were handled individually), which in time reached the United States Supreme Court. Although Liebowitz had been told about the ILD's ideology and methods, he could not at first believe that the organization would put political and propaganda concerns so far above the immediate legal interests of the defendants. Gradually, however, it dawned upon him what the ILD was up to, whereupon he withdrew, denouncing the ILD for its machinations and calling attention to the fact that in the name of Scottsboro it had raised large sums of money, presumably for defense purposes, and then diverted it to wholly unrelated party activities. Liebowitz had handled the case without compensation. While he was still the counsel of record, the ILD began to subject him to biting criticism.[17]

During the period from 1931 to 1935 the Scottsboro case received almost continuous attention in the Communist press; the party never let pass any opportunity to belabor the NAACP and its leaders for their insistence that nonrevolutionary approaches to the courts were the essential—in fact, the only— paths to racial justice. The invective heaped on the Association and its leaders reached a new high in volume and intensity. By 1935, however, the ILD was prepared to make overtures to the NAACP and other Negro organizations concerning the Scottsboro case, which was still plodding through the courts while the accused remained in prison.[18] The move was dictated not by a belief that some cooperative endeavor of the two

[17] *Ibid.*, pp. 277–278.
[18] Editorial, "Betrayal by the NAACP," *New Masses*, XIV (Jan. 8, 1935), 6.

organizations would possibly free the boys; it was a result of two factors that have not been accorded the attention they deserve in the voluminous literature on Scottsboro. These were the beginning of a shift in the Communist Party line from dual, separatist, revolutionary action to nondirect, nonviolent, "united front" endeavors in concert with moderate and leftist movements, and the fact that the law of diminishing political and propaganda returns had set in for that particular issue. At one time many Negroes were inclined to believe that the ILD's concern for the defendants was genuine and that its methods were appropriate, perhaps even necessary; accordingly, they contributed money and other kinds of support. Eventually they began to raise questions about the noisy talk, the aggressive gestures, the appeals for more money—and the few concrete results. The Communists could not go on indefinitely appealing for sacrifices when consequences that Negroes expected—and could understand—were so few. Scottsboro had thus become something of a liability for the CP and the ILD.

Meanwhile the NAACP had fought the ILD, pointing out time and again the nature of the latter's interest in the case, calling attention to the misuse of defense funds, and insisting that the cause of racial justice could but fail when judicial processes were linked to revolutionary aims and became secondary to political purpose. One obviously cannot simultaneously pursue and denounce established legal procedures; how can serious appeals be made when the appellants are at the same time denying that the courts can act independently of political considerations? Although the Association's desire to free the defendants was never dampened, its hands were tied during the very time when legal appeals should have been pushed most vigorously through the courts. When a new coalition of organizations was formed in 1935 to try again to win acquittal, the NAACP went along even though the coalition included the ILD. The new Scottsboro Defense Committee included representatives of the American Civil Liberties Union, the Methodist Federation for Social Action, the Socialist League for Industrial Democracy, the Church League for Industrial Democracy, and the National Urban League (representatives of the latter served in an unofficial capacity), as well as the NAACP and the ILD. Significantly, it was the moderate organizations, especially the NAACP, that were responsible for the new round of long and involved court appeals and negotiations with Alabama officials which eventually led to freedom for most of the defendants. The CP and the ILD welcomed the outcome, which could be interpreted as verification of the "united front" approach, and which diverted attention from the failure of the Communists to accomplish anything by themselves. Later the Stalinists were to revive memories of the Scottsboro case, using them as a means of attacking the NAACP and the NUL in the post-World War II period.

The NAACP's cooperation with the ILD on the last push to free the Scottsboro defendants was not the forerunner of a new era of peace and harmony. Like the child once burned who is afraid of fire, the NAACP viewed the sudden change of party heart with skepticism. Association leaders feared the party's embrace more than its enmity, for they foresaw new party efforts (1) to infiltrate local branches by pointing to cooperation at the top, (2) to form local front groups for which NAACP members would be courted, and (3) to gain respectability for party causes by pointing to the party's new allies in the Scottsboro case. Torn between such risks and a genuine interest in the nine defendants, the NAACP reluctantly joined the coalition.

The period of the United Front will be dealt with in detail in the next chapter. Before that time arrived the party continued to lambaste the NAACP, its foremost rival for Negro allegiance, and other reformist Negro organizations as well.

The Communists attempted to discredit such agencies among their own followers and to undermine their frequently tenuous structures. Establishing rival organizations in whatever areas of Negro life the party thought might be penetrated, it tried to widen schisms within the Negro community and to capitalize the class, color, and social differences it found there.

The indigenous reformist groups were struggling with internal and external crises of the first magnitude. Lacking both the funds and the organizational apparatus for dealing with the major economic problems confronting most Negroes, the NAACP nearly went under. It was prepared to work slowly and carefully on such matters as education, voting, housing, and civil rights for Negroes, but it was poorly equipped to tackle mass unemployment and its myriad consequences. For many Negroes, including even some in the relatively small middle-class group, the basic problems were now those of physical survival and maintenance of a modicum of social and psychological well-being in the face of immense, impersonal, dislocating economic forces.

Lower-strata Negroes encountered in more intensified form the old problems of getting a job, enough to eat, and a place to live, so as to keep the family together. Highly disproportionate numbers of Negroes were unemployed, underemployed, without housing, on relief. They had never been particularly attracted to the Association; now the kind of issues the NAACP had been struggling with—breaking the white primary, gaining admittance to graduate schools, defending individual rights in the courts—seemed even further removed from the common colored man's world of reality. Even so, the lower classes probably weathered the depression better socially and psychologically than did the middle class, which found its hard-won respectability ebbing away as the prosperity of the twenties receded. As rural Negroes sometimes put it, "Them that ain't flew so high ain't got so far to fall." The NAACP could offer neither group a real solution.

In reacting to the depression the NAACP was characteristically slow. Its leaders were hesitant. But if they knew not what to do or how to do it, they had for company the American Federation of Labor, the Chamber of Commerce, and the President of the United States. Some kinds of crises in American life have provided opportunities as well as problems. The crisis of war, for example, had in the past offered colored workers a chance to improve their bargaining position in the tightening labor market. Crises also had precipitated Negro migrations to areas where there was greater personal freedom, social opportunity, and political participation and fewer restraints by law, tradition, and racial prejudice. The result had been a changed outlook, with Negroes seeing more clearly the nature of the gap between professed democratic ideals and existing racial practices. Although Negroes had received less than any other group from the society they had been called upon to defend in war, they had viewed war, as had other disadvantaged minorities, in terms of both sacrifice and new horizons. World War I, for example, had demonstrated that they could do as well as the next man when the avenues of opportunity were opened. Perhaps that fact helps to account for the virtual absence of pacifist sentiment among colored Americans in World Wars I and II, though there was also the feeling that Negroes, until recently politically powerless, could do little to shape the main drift of national policy and should make the best of the white man's war, if he insisted on having it.

A depression, or even a limited recession, is a different kind of crisis. The NAACP rolls withered rather than fattened during the early years of the depression decade. Marxist theory might have it that the ranks of the poor should close and tighten in

69

unity when capitalism falters and economic catastrophe strikes; correlatively, prosperity might be supposed to dispel unity as proletarians find they can make it alone. In the actual case just the opposite is true. Unions and other ameliorative organizations have waxed in boom and waned in slump, at least in the United States. When the economy is healthy and opportunity levels are high, prodding and pressuring by reformist groups get results; dissenters' hopes are high; and there is money to pay dues. When a great depression strikes, the problem of survival is so pressing as to blot out other issues, and the gradualist, piecemeal programs of groups such as the NAACP fall into ineffectuality. An unemployed Negro need not be a Marxist in order to act like an economic determinist.

Until the depression struck, the Association's concern for the franchise, residential segregation, equal education, and civil rights, reflecting the values of the Negro middle class and the elitist outlook of its leaders, took the capitalist order for granted. Specifically rejected was the Communist contention that racial prejudice was peculiar to a given stage of economic development and could be overcome only when capitalism was abolished.

Even prior to the general depression, the Negro's economic position was largely marginal because of a concentration of the black population in the rural South, where agricultural crisis was chronic. There, in the 1920's, Negroes were being edged out of what skilled and semiskilled jobs they had managed to secure, while the hoped-for break in the dreary cycle of sharecropping and farm tenancy, leading to eventual independent land ownership, never materialized. Depression developments drove even deeper wedges between Negro and white workers. The 1930 convention of the Association indicated some awareness of the rapid impact of the burgeoning depression on Negro welfare. However, its leaders, along with Mr. Hoover, seemed to feel—or hope—that prosperity was no further away than the next corner. The resolutions adopted mirrored certain misgivings about the ability to achieve full citizenship in the absence of minimum economic security. But the means for attaining the latter objective were not explored with rigor.

With the depression deepening, the 1931 convention of the Association took a more questioning and inclusive view of the problems affecting Negroes. For the first time a forthright call for the alliance of Negroes with organized labor, qualified only by the demand that the latter's racial barriers be dropped, was issued, indicating quite a shift in outlook. However, the leaders remained uncertain about the specific things to be done. Even in 1932 the Association was prepared to go no further than the general dictum that Negroes and white workers faced common problems calling for a common, cooperative solution. One thing was clear: the inability of the Association to go it alone, even in the action areas where it had presumably perfected its approach and techniques. It needed allies. But where to turn? The trade-unions were something less than eager for racial cooperation, and the CP, before the United Front period, would have responded favorably only on the condition of complete capitulation by the NAACP. As a means of wringing concessions from the white community, NAACP leaders issued caveats about the possibility of Negroes turning "radical" if their plight was not alleviated; but this was an ancient stratagem, and those who voiced the warning scarcely believed it themselves.

The Association's leaders were committed to maintaining the NAACP as a continuing force in Negro life while keeping its structure intact and their own positions secure. That was understandable in men who equated race welfare with the welfare of the NAACP. To have embraced economic radicalism would have meant indictment of the very class on whose support the Association depended. Even so mild a thing as hinting that the NAACP might well make overtures to the labor movement caused some rumblings among conservative members, especially the Negro professionals and businessmen.

During that time Du Bois gave expression through the columns of *Crisis* to a ferment within the NAACP hierarchy. He demanded that the Association identify itself more closely with the mass of Negroes, a rather striking proposal from the originator and personal embodiment of the Talented Tenth concept. Going further, he called for decentralization of the NAACP's internal structure, with more autonomy for local branches. He wanted the annual convention rather than the self-perpetuating Executive Board to be the final arbiter of policy. Moreover, he was disturbed by the Association's lack of concern about foreign affairs, particularly relations with the colonial peoples of Africa and Asia; he wanted the NAACP to commit itself unequivocally to their liberation. Finally, he demanded that the NAACP appeal more effectively to younger Negroes and intellectuals.[19]

While the Du Bois proposals bore rather close outward resemblance to those advocated at the time by the Communists, they were original with Du Bois. He did not link them to an over-all theory of history or social change. If implemented, they might have caused a radical transformation of the NAACP, but he regarded them as nothing more than pragmatic solutions for immediate organizational and racial issues. Such similarity as they had to the party's offerings were a matter of coincidence. The *Crisis* editor was voicing misgivings and demands which were less forcefully put but perhaps just as keenly felt by other members of the Association. Significantly, at the very time he was advocating those measures, Du Bois was under almost continuous attack from the CP.

On economic matters Du Bois' proposals were something of a throwback to Garvey and Washington. He suggested that Negroes make a group effort to hold their present employment

[19] Lawrence, *op. cit.*, p. 138.

and pool their resources to start new all-Negro businesses. Economic separatism was combined with racial radicalism in his plan to form Negro group-purchasing institutions and a Negro economic "general staff" to develop an independent racial economic life in the United States. At the same time Negroes were to continue to press for full civil and social rights. Some of his organizational proposals were later adopted in watered-down form, but the Association's leaders, who have always been primarily integrationists, rejected his separatist economic measures. By continuing to advocate the latter he incurred increasing disfavor, which partly led to his resignation in 1934.

A lateral development to Du Bois' economic separatism was found in the "Don't Buy Where You Can't Work" movement, which caught on in a number of cities during that period. The NAACP preferred to remain aloof from such campaigns. However, they were popular among northern urban Negroes and at times received the backing of local NAACP branches. The national officers considered it expedient to "go along," realizing that otherwise they might alienate members who saw concrete changes resulting from this form of direct action, from which they derived a sense of effectiveness. They sensed also that Negro extremists, left and right, would attempt to capitalize the issue. Even in the 1960's, sporadic campaigns, such as the San Francisco branch's effort to obtain jobs for Negro drivers in the Yellow Cab Company, receive official support from the national office.

During the depression it became increasingly clear that the race's economic problems would have to be dealt with primarily by political means. Whereas the Association's political participation had been spotty in the past, by 1932 the plight of Negroes was so desperate that a reluctance to use politics on a systematic and sustained basis was largely overcome. The Association was concerned not only that Negroes have the

73

right to vote but also that they use their franchise to support reform measures of benefit to lower-strata groups generally and to Negroes in particular. While maintaining its nonpartisan pose, the NAACP strongly supported Roosevelt and most of the ensuing New Deal relief and employment measures from which Negroes benefited disproportionately because they had been hardest hit. Here was an indication of firm commitment to pragmatic, and often liberal, political action. Again, however, the development was sparked not by the Communists or other Marxian-oriented groups, or by radical ideologies, but by day-to-day experiences of Negroes and the Association's need to come up with a program adequate for the challenge.

Indeed, until about 1936 the CP was a vociferous critic of Roosevelt and his reform measures. The Communists believed rightly that the man in the White House and his wife had cut much of the ground from under the party's propaganda appeals to Negroes. The Communists' opposition to the early New Deal, which brought Negroes their first real measure of relief, was based partly on a recognition that colored citizens would turn to radicalism only as a last, desperate measure. The Communist shift in 1935 moved the Stalinists' immediate political outlook closer to that of the average Negro—not the other way around. Although Negroes at last had broken with the Republican Party, which could exploit the Lincoln legend only so far, they did not move to the opposite extreme and identify with radical political movements.

Even where Negroes did respond tentatively to Communist organizations—among the unemployed, sharecroppers, workers, and intellectuals—there was a pronounced tendency to conceive objectives in immediate, pragmatic terms, definitions which the party momentarily accepted and acted on. In contrast to the moderate organizations, the Communists were willing and to some extent able to work among the lower-strata Negroes on a grass-roots basis, organizing unemployed councils, relief demonstrations, hunger marches, and protests. This was plodding, unscintillating work, calling for dedicated acolytes who truly believed the future lay with the working classes. The party could staff such campaigns better than could the NAACP, for obvious reasons. The ideological commitments of most Negroes participating in the actions were limited, tenuous, and lacking in a broader sophistication the party would have welcomed. But though the Negro in distress could not grasp the finer points of Communist doctrine, he could understand the slogans for more relief, the halting of evictions, and the availability of more jobs with higher pay in public-works programs. And if he found himself associating with the Communists on those terms, he was nonetheless disinclined to make an over-all commitment to the party's larger objectives.

Understandably, NAACP leaders were disturbed by efforts of the party to capitalize the Negro's plight. They were convinced that once the stirring-up was done with, little would remain in the way of concrete gains, and that the noise itself was the main objective. Equally important, however, was a fear that Communist-led movements would challenge the Association itself, threatening both its ideological base and its organizational structure. Realistically, perhaps, NAACP spokesmen feared not the radicalism but the susceptibility of the Negro masses, who might fall in behind the red banner of James Ford as they had earlier followed the black flag of Garvey. In that respect Association officials voiced a sentiment that is one of the historic traits of both the conservative and the ultraradical: the masses must be held in check and led by elites.

The halting and inconsistent steps the NAACP took on various issues underscored the difficulties in modifying its traditional program and developing a suitable apparatus. Yet the pressures to do so remained strong. That the organization was able to shift, however slowly, is testimony to the flexibility of its leaders and to the value of intraorganizational conflict as an antidote to stagnation. The interaction between what John Roche has termed the "enthusiasts" and the "bureaucrats," although a source of personal animosities, was also the locus of organizational adaptability.

Without doubt, the CP influenced the NAACP in a number of indirect ways, as, indeed, it was to influence other organizations, for example, the trade-unions. The shifts within the Association were in part a response to the party's challenge; had they occurred sooner, the party's influence, such as it was among Negroes, would have been even more limited. Here and there the party demonstrated that lower-strata Negroes could be aroused and organized around immediate issues. It showed that racial discontent could be turned to political account, particularly when underscored by economic catastrophe. Although the party was unable to build a mass Negro following, it approached a stratum of the race frequently regarded by the NAACP as the middle-class Negro's burden. More sophisticated than their rank and file and having a personal identity with the Association, NAACP leaders showed little inclination to sever old ties to join a movement that was as unpredictable as it was radical. Significantly, no top or intermediate leader of the Association, as far as has been determined, defected to the party during that period, and no Communist held any position of consequence in the national office.

Authority in the NAACP was centralized in the Executive Board, which controlled the selection of the executive secretary and the rest of the national staff; indeed, the Board could hire and fire at will without accounting to the membership. Given the composition of the membership at that time, however, it is highly unlikely that it would have approved Communists for any important posts. The Association could not afford to be too restrictive about the political coloration of mere members, however, since they were hard to come by.

Criticism by Negro newspapers and young intellectuals was yet another force pushing the NAACP toward a broadened program. In the spring of 1932 Du Bois polled seventeen editors of leading papers about communism and the activities of the party among Negroes. Carl Murphy of the *Baltimore Afro-American* praised the party for its insistence on internal racial equality and its concern for the plight of lower-strata Negroes. William M. Kelly of the *Amsterdam News* voiced agreement in principle with what he described as Communist objectives in the race field but expressed serious doubts concerning their practicability in the United States. Young of the *Norfolk Journal and Guide* and Dungee of the *Black Dispatch* (Oklahoma) conceded that the Communists had made some contribution to Negro betterment but emphasized the party's limitations and questioned its final objectives. Five of the editors voiced the opinion that communism was making some headway among Negroes but saw no cause for alarm, since the party's influence was predicated on immediate issues and Negroes showed little concern for its ultimate objectives. Frank M. Davis, editor of the *Atlanta Daily World*, held that the party was making few gains among Negroes. Although glad that that was the case, he did not condemn the Communists outright. In contrast, Willis Cole of the *Louisville Leader* felt that the party was making serious inroads and deplored what he thought was a widespread favorable response to Communist appeals. Two editors, Robert L. Vann (*Pittsburgh Courier*) and Fred R. Moore (*New York Age*), condemned the party roundly, expressing the hope that Negroes would steer entirely clear of it.[20]

That few of the Negro newsmen were wholly critical of the party was an eye opener for the NAACP. In a sense their responses were back-handed slaps at the Association, whose

[20] *Ibid.*, pp. 174–178.

frailties became more apparent as the depression deepened. NAACP officials could hardly afford to ignore the opinions and implied recommendations of such influential race spokesmen. It must be kept in mind, however, that the editors' responses were intended for white eyes and ears as well, by indirection suggesting that Negroes would seek radical alternatives if their most pressing needs were not met.

In 1933 the discontent of young colored intellectuals with the NAACP was brought to the fore at the second Amenia Conference, the first having been held in 1916. Some forty prominent young Negroes participated in the sessions held on the Spingarn estate in New York. Present also were a number of the "elders," including NAACP officials. The latter were shocked at the critical mood and the radical reactions of their would-be protégés. Although there were diverse views among the younger set, there was general agreement that large-scale, militant political and economic action was the best means for improving the position of the Negro. Implicit was the assumption that the old guard didn't have the answers.[21]

Time and again the NAACP was criticized by the conference for its exclusiveness, hesitancy, conservatism, and shortsightedness. There were charges of reluctance to undertake mass organization among Negroes and of too slavish adherence to time-honored and timeworn tactics which were no longer sufficient. But though young Amenia participants were racially militant and showed a surprising acquaintance with Marxian theories and movements, few of them were Communists. Growing up in a political and social environment different from that of their elders, vicitimized by the depression, operating in a context of institutional as well as personal crisis, and seeking positions of racial leadership, they were understandably unhappy with the ineffectual role being played by the NAACP in the great drama taking place before them. But to whom could they turn and what could they do?

[21] Bunche, *op. cit.*, pp. 209–210.

Marxism, emerging from the immigrant ghettos in the 1930's, began to reach the colleges and universities, even the Negro campuses in the South. Not many colored students turned True Believer, but some were influenced by the Communists' explanation of the old order in crisis and were responsive to its emphasis on economic forces as the root of most, if not all, evil. Some students wished to rally the black masses to a new faith and lead them along a leftward-curving road to salvation. Yet few of them paused, at Amenia or elsewhere, to consider that they themselves were neither from nor of the masses. Indeed, in acquiring intellectual status, they had increased the barrier between themselves and those they would lead. Since few had yet wet their feet in organizing the lower echelons, their innocence was virtually intact; the thought that sharecroppers and coal miners might not come rushing into the fold if invited to do so was submerged in the general enthusiasm.

There is a temptation, from the perspective of the 1960's, to treat the concern of those young militants for the masses with condescension or contempt. The fact that their enthusiasm came to little should not enhance the temptation. Unsuccessful radicals do not write the accepted histories. But before the Amenia insurgents are cavalierly dismissed, one might pause to honor them for having embodied in their own time and in their own way the "dissident impulse" in American life, an impulse whose lack of vitality in the present era undergirds a stultifying conformity.

In any event, the stir which the "young Turks" caused at Amenia was duplicated in other places where the elders gathered with youths to discuss problems of the race in the early 1930's. The discontent of the angry young men almost always included criticism of the NAACP, whose leaders accepted with few qualifications the existing capitalist order as a framework within which racial rights could be won. By late 1933 the NAACP leaders, while retaining their ideological focus, were changing their emphasis and broadening their sights. They insisted that their response was autonomous and predicated on a calm analysis of the scene, but there can be little doubt that the Amenia needle prick had struck blood.

Structurally the NAACP remained much the same, with real authority still vested in the Executive Board, though a few concessions were made to internal criticism and outside pressure. The concessions—for example, some of the critics were put on the Board—only whetted the appetite of the dissenters for a more thorough overhaul. The annual conference held in St. Louis in June, 1935, was publicized in advance as a turning point in the Association's history. It was thought that the conference would broaden and make official the adaptations of the past several years. In particular it was believed that prolonged criticism of the oligarchic apparatus would culminate in steps to provide real internal democracy with greater autonomy for local branches. The advocates of reform represented varying shades of political opinion, including radical intellectuals. Although their discontent reflected some Communist infiltration and pressure, the unrest was largely indigenous.

Much of the discontent cut across regional and political lines. However, it was never effectively centered in a disciplined group or articulated by a recognized spokesman. Some dissenters criticized the Association on its own ground; specifically they claimed that even in its chosen field, the prosecution of civil rights cases, the NAACP had fallen short of any acceptable mark.

The NAACP leaders, it had been conjectured beforehand, would accept some rather thoroughgoing changes at St. Louis. Membership was still only 85,000; dues were insufficient for the tasks at hand. Negro intellectuals were beginning to be disenchanted and could no longer be counted on to perform their ideological and agitational roles for the NAACP. Rival organizations, especially the left-wing groups, were making a lot of noise among the white-collar and industrial workers as well as among the tenants and sharecroppers in the South. While the Association's leaders went along with many of the reformers' economic and political proposals and even spoke in behalf of them, they in characteristic bureaucratic fashion did not relinquish their grip on the national office or extend branch autonomy or divest the self-perpetuating Executive Board of final authority on policy matters. The critics appeared to have won a victory if judged from the resolutions adopted, but the reins were still held firmly in the same old hands.

J. E. Spingarn, white philanthropist who had been one of the Association's founders and who acted as spokesman for the officialdom, insisted on a gradualist approach, stressing the difficulties inherent in carrying out the new economic and political program called for by the convention. He launched a vigorous attack on the Communists, warning delegates not to associate with them and calling attention to the party's designs on the NAACP. Fear of Communist infiltration of local branches or of the defection of Association members to the party was an important factor in retaining the centralized organizational structure and continuing the restraints on local branches. If the party could capture enough branches and if the locus of policy were shifted from the Board to the convention, the Communists could conceivably control the organization. The fear, though not wholly imaginary, was overdrawn. Of at least equal importance in the leaders' eagerness to retain the existing power structure was their belief that by experience, knowledge, personal dedication, and long commitment to the NAACP they were the natural guardians of the Association's welfare. In typical bureaucratic fashion, the incumbent officialdom identified its own interests with those of the organization. The Board had no intention of diluting its power, and dissenters at St. Louis could either go along or withdraw from the NAACP.

The party's attitude toward the Association was not immediately modified. The Communists kept up their attack through the party, the ILD, the LSNR, and other organizations. Even as the United Front was being launched during that year, the Stalinists could find little to justify inclusion of the NAACP, assuming that the Association, like Barkis, was willing. However, by the end of 1935 the United Front was in full swing, and the CP was finally willing to extend the left hand of fellowship to an organization which only a few months before it had denounced as a hopeless supporter of "imperialist reaction" and a saboteur of the "mass aspirations of the Negro people."

The gains the CP made from 1929 to 1935 were realized primarily on issues of everyday importance; the response of Negroes could rarely be projected into visions of a new society. In fact, to keep the picture in focus, one must remember that the party's following among Negroes was disproportionately low. The party's strength, such as it was, rested chiefly on its ability to appeal ideologically to a few Negro intellectuals and to stir some lower-strata Negroes on immediate issues.

From the standpoint of membership the NAACP was somewhat better off at the close of the six-year period than at the beginning, though its coffers were far from full. So far as concerns influence, particularly outside the Negro community, it had made gains. The improvement was a result in part of the general upsurge of reform that came with the New Deal. Ameliorative groups had become respectable in the general ferment of the Roosevelt era, and the NAACP's public image brightened accordingly. There was official recognition of its voice as a spokesman for the Negro's aspirations, and its leaders found men of power in Washington more accessible.

By turning, however slowly, to economic and political action, the NAACP was beginning to develop promising organizational skills whose value was to be demonstrated time and again during the following three decades. Having undergone an organizational crisis, a part of which flowed from efforts by the Communists to destroy it, the Association emerged with a somewhat broader vision, increased political sophistication, and restored confidence in its ability to function as an agency of racial protest. What impresses one as paradoxical is the fact that the NAACP weathered both organizational and racial crises with few ideological and structural changes. It might be argued that if NAACP leaders had been more imaginative in going to the masses, had taken the wraps off local units, had fired the hopes of the intellectuals, and had mapped out a comprehensive blueprint of the good society, they might have accomplished more. Unfortunately, there is no way of testing such conditionals conclusively, and the student is left with the possibility that just the opposite might have been the result.

The period 1929 to 1935 may be viewed as one in which differences between the NAACP and the CP became increasingly clear, erupting in open conflict in Scottsboro and a few other places. The differences were fought out also in the columns of the *New Masses* and the *Daily Worker* and on the pages of *Crisis* and *Opportunity*. Eventually they would have to be fought out in the minds of thoughtful Negroes; but that would come in a later era. What is perhaps most significant about those years, given the crisis in Negro life and the energetic efforts of the CP to win black men to its cause, is that so many Negroes chose, either positively or by default, the course charted by the NAACP.

IV

The United Front
and World War II

THE rise of Hitler and certain developments within the Soviet Union caused the Comintern to inaugurate the United
Front strategy beginning in late 1933. The Communist Party
in the United States, after a good deal of fumbling and halting, fell into line and tried with some success to translate the
new directives into action. The new look required renuncia-
tion of the program followed during the immediately preceding period and, of course, a different approach to Negroes
and non-Communist Negro organizations, whose cooperation
the party now needed.[1]

Of special interest to the student of race and politics is
the relationship between the Communist movement and the
NAACP during the several years in which the party proclaimed
that communism was "Twentieth-Century Americanism."
Whereas the party had regarded the Association as its arch-
enemy in the field of race relations during the preceding
period, the abrupt change in line led Communists to tone
down their attacks and even to seek alliance with the NAACP
on specific issues.

[1] For a detailed account of international developments as they
dictated this shift, see W. Record, *op. cit.*, pp. 52–64.

Communists sometimes expressed an inability to understand why the NAACP leaders hung back. However, the Communists' new pitch to the Association had been helped not at all by the disclosure in August, 1935, that the USSR had provided oil, food, and other supplies to Mussolini for his Ethiopian venture. *Crisis* attacked editorially both the USSR and the CP for pretending to be champions of downtrodden black people in Africa while at the same time reaping a neat profit from dealing with an imperialist power bent on their subjugation. Such patent cynicism shocked not only the NAACP, in spite of its familiarity with the opportunism of the party, but other Negro organizations as well. Even in the party's own organizations, Negro members found it difficult to accept the labored rationalizations of Soviet behavior offered by William L. Patterson, Harry Gannes, and Earl Browder. Herman W. Mackawain, the acting secretary of the still-functioning League of Struggle for Negro Rights, resigned in disgust, denouncing the CP and the USSR, although a long-standing discontent with the party and some of its leaders in New York also contributed to his final break.

The NAACP's criticism was especially pointed and revealed how mistrustful its leaders were of new Communist overtures. *Crisis* editorialized:

Of course, close students of Soviet Russia discovered long ago that the great idealism of the so-called Communist nation was in reality hard-boiled opportunism, and opportunism as shameless as that of any nation not professing the high idealism preached by the Kremlin. Therefore it is only recording one more inconsistency and not one more surprise to set down that the Soviets are raking in good capitalist profits selling wheat and coal tar to Italy for use in the war against Ethiopia.

We have little quarrel with the Soviet pursuit of profits—even imperialist war profits. Business men are business men whether their offices are on Red Square in Moscow or Wall Street in

New York. We do not object to the pious flub-dub sported by Communists such as: "love for the downtrodden," "self-determination for small nations," "fight imperialist war," etc. They are always ranting about capitalist exploitation and robbery and drawing themselves up in their pet holier-than-thou attitude, but whenever the opportunity presents itself they are in the midst of the arms and munitions races, military alliances and in garnering of profits.[4]

Communists tried hard in succeeding months to push the Ethiopian issue, or at least Soviet aid to Mussolini, into the background. But the NAACP never permitted them to forget it, plaguing the Stalinists with sharp reminders throughout the United Front period and with freshened criticism when Stalin made another opportunistic deal with the Nazis in 1939.

The NAACP found itself confronting the party in the field of trade-unionism as the CIO's organizing drive spread to the mass-production industries and gained momentum. By that time the Association had come to accept the desirability, indeed the necessity, of cooperating with the labor movement, especially the new CIO organizations, which proclaimed a policy of nondiscrimination in those industries employing the bulk of Negro industrial workers—steel, automobiles, mining, meat packing, rubber, and others. The National Urban League had come to the same realization, and as early as 1934 it organized workers' councils aimed at educating Negroes to an acceptance of and participation in the labor movement.[5]

The NAACP, after a brief skeptical period, was soon urging Negro workers to support the CIO groups and to press for

[4] *Crisis,* XLII (Oct., 1935), 305; Nolan, *op. cit.,* p. 135.

[5] Lester B. Granger, testimony, House Committee on Un-American Activities, *Hearings regarding Communist Infiltration of Minority Groups* (Part I), July 14, 1949, 81st Cong., 1st sess., p. 467. Granger and other Negro spokesmen asked to testify following Paul Robeson's charge, made in Paris, that Negroes would not support a war against the USSR.

88

equal rights within them. The Association's leaders, although somewhat divided on that issue as they were on others, were aware that the party was active in some of the unions. They knew that John L. Lewis had accepted Communist help in organizing the CIO and that the party had brought blocs of members in from the old TUUL affiliates. They were aware, too, that party functionaries had made their way into some key posts in the organizing committees, from which they later worked to gain control of the permanent organizations.

The NAACP, however, was hardly in a position to urge Negro industrial workers to avoid union participation because they might meet some Communists. To have done so would have been to estrange even further the lower-strata Negroes whom the Association was increasingly eager to reach. Further, the NAACP needed the moral and organizational support of the new unions. Association leaders would think twice before either ignoring or opposing a movement that attacked not only racial discrimination in industry but also the economic and political problems of all American workers. The CIO accepted NAACP cooperation, emphasizing common interests of the two organizations. Unlike the CP, the CIO did not secretly regard the destruction of the Association as a condition for its success among Negroes. Quite the contrary.[6]

There was some risk that, in aligning itself with the CIO, the NAACP would antagonize the leaders of the AFL and thus jeopardize the limited support that group had given the Association in the past. But the NAACP could ill afford not to identify itself with a movement that challenged racial segregation in those industries where many Negroes worked. Indeed, the NAACP saw a chance to use the rivalry between the AFL and the CIO as a means of forcing modifications in the racially restrictive policies of the Federation's affiliates. The AFL became more receptive to the pleas of such men as A. Philip

[6] NAACP, *Labor Manual* (New York: NAACP, 1957), p. 58.

Randolph for at least some innovations in the exclusionist policies of many of its organizations. For since Negroes now had meaningful choices in selecting bargaining representatives, they were in a position to demand rights rather than request privileges from the older unions. Even so, the AFL moved slowly; as a consequence, it forfeited many potential Negro members.

The NAACP's acceptance of the new unionism was evidenced in various ways. Association publications urged Negroes to sign up. Negro labor leaders such as Willard Townsend and A. Philip Randolph were invited into the NAACP councils. Later Walter Reuther and Philip Murray became members of the Executive Board. Significantly, all four men were known anti-Communists, although they had found it expedient on occasion to restrain their feelings so as not to hamper drives to organize the unorganized.

Resolutions at the annual conventions further reflected the NAACP's new concern for unionism. Labor spokesmen appeared in growing numbers as delegates and were given prominent places on the programs. Labor leaders were consulted with increasing frequency by the Executive Board in the formulation of Association policies. At the community level branches cooperated with the CIO organizing committees and with newly established local unions. In the political arena the NAACP, without taking an official position, worked closely with the unions to elect Democratic candidates, or the more liberal Republicans; in the South, of course, the Association supported those Democrats who had the least offensive record on race and union issues. In following that program the Association had to overcome considerable internal resistance, especially among local branch leaders whose skepticism of unions, even the new CIO units, ran deep and was understandable in view of the middle-class character of most NAACP local officials and the long anti-Negro record of the old-line labor movement. NAACP members in industry had a more direct mistrust of unions, based on the fact that frequently in the past they had been able to gain employment only over the strong protests and sometimes the figurative dead bodies of white unionists.

Even when Negro workers had been ill-used by employers —discharged precipitately after serving as strikebreakers, for example, or assigned the lowest jobs—there persisted a tendency to identify with management rather than with the unions. Colored workers in the Ford plants were a good example. Winning them was essential to unionizing the company; in the process the CIO-NAACP relationship was strongly reinforced. Ford had given Negroes the heaviest, dirtiest work in the plants; most worked in the foundry. Yet they were strongly loyal to Ford, for he *had* given them jobs—and more money than they knew existed before they migrated from the cotton fields of the South. Colored workers were Ford's strongest bulwark against the union, and Ford was the hardest nut for the CIO's automobile workers' organizing drive to crack. The new cooperation between the NAACP and the unions was exemplified by the dramatic appearance of Walter White beside Walter Reuther in Detroit to appeal to Negro workers to join the CIO.

Finding it inexpedient to attack the Communists in the CIO directly, the NAACP sought to offset their influence in a number of ways. It brought non-Communist labor leaders into closer contact with its own officers and members. It cooperated closely with other non-Communist organizations, such as the Socialist League for Industrial Democracy, that were active in the industrial unionism campaign. The national office maintained a closer watch on the branches to protect them against party infiltration, now made easier by the "new look" of the comrades and the receptiveness of units to labor spokesmen.

The Executive Board established a labor division in the national office, part of its responsibility being to keep the officers informed of party activities in unions and to check on local branches where CP penetration by its labor activists was a possibility. Going further, the NAACP aided the establishment of Negro caucuses within the new unions, encouraging black members to be more active and to press for a fair racial shake while being on the alert for party skulduggery. There was no NAACP intent to build Negro voting blocs within the unions; that device, however, the Communists did employ, sometimes successfully. The NAACP did press the unions, old and new, to establish internal fair practice committees to eliminate discrimination within specific unions and industries. If Negro workers could thus be assured that their interests were being guarded, there was less likelihood that they would turn to the Communists, who were more than willing to pose as their champions.[7]

The party might have been more successful in penetrating the NAACP, using union members as the infiltrators, had it made an all-out effort to do so. But after all, the party was approaching the pinnacle of its strength while the Association was still reorienting itself toward political and economic action; Communists did not then believe the NAACP had the makings of a mass organization. Many more Negroes, they thought, could be reached effectively through the new trade-unions and their political apparatus, in which the party had influence. Their economic determinism reinforced by the depression experience, the Communists put faith in Negro workers as the backbone of any large racial movement and concentrated efforts directly on Negroes in unions rather than in the NAACP per se. It was thus that they fought the Association for influence among the black workers. In line with the over-all

[7] Irving Howe and B. J. Widick, *The UAW and Walter Reuther* (New York: Random House, 1949), pp. 223–235 and chap. x.

United Front program, which emphasized cooperation with existing organizations willing to endorse and perhaps work actively on specific domestic and foreign issues, Communists hoped that the NAACP would tag along and that its leaders might be won over or neutralized if their organization was not attacked directly but "guided" along the proper course.

Finally, Communists wanted to build a mass United Front of the Negro People by bringing together in a single body the trade-union, protest, betterment, welfare, religious, and political organizations. Success required, if not the enthusiastic support, at least the neutrality of the NAACP. Neither could be obtained if the Communists pushed their "boring from within" or frontal assault tactics too far, placing the Association leaders on the defensive and antagonizing the rank and file.

Such calculated restraint informed Communist involvement in organizing the National Negro Congress (NNC), which convened in Chicago in February, 1936. In large part the NNC was a result of efforts of the Joint Committee on National Recovery (JCNR), which had been formed in the early days of the New Deal to protect the interests of Negroes in the many new government agencies. Composed of representatives of twenty-two Negro organizations, the JCNR received the bulk of its operating funds from the NAACP, another indication of the latter's shift to a political-action orientation. Communist organizations were not invited to the first assemblies of the JCNR, although some of the principal delegates, such as John P. Davis, were identified with the party or in sympathy with it. (Davis' commitment was to become quite apparent in 1939 when he endorsed the virtual liquidation of the NNC and helped maneuver the remains into the hands of the party.[8])

In the spring of 1935 the JCNR sponsored at Howard University a conference which reviewed a wide range of Negro

[8] Bunche, *op. cit.*, pp. 370–371.

problems and explored ways and means of dealing with them. Out of the deliberations, in which some representatives of Communist organizations had participated, came a proposal to form a broadly based national Negro agency comprising economic, political, fraternal, religious, protest, and welfare groups. A special committee was set up to organize a national Negro congress; John P. Davis, who had served as chairman of the JCNR, was to be organizer-secretary.

The sponsoring committee for the congress secured the support of such prominent non-Communists as Lester Granger of the Urban League, A. Philip Randolph of the Brotherhood of Sleeping Car Porters, M. O. Bousfield of the Julius Rosenwald Fund, and W. J. Walls, a Methodist bishop. The endorsements, however, did not imply official approval by organizations the men represented. The NAACP remained skeptical and somewhat aloof, one reason being that James W. Ford, the CP's vice-presidential candidate in 1932 and a former organizer of the party's TUUL, was a member of the organizing committee. Without doubt some organizational jealousy was also involved.

Ford made one of the principal speeches at the organizing convention in Chicago, which adopted a series of resolutions calling for opposition to war and fascism, more civil rights for Negroes, improvement of the conditions of colored sharecroppers, organization of Negroes into industrial unions, mass racial consumer cooperatives, and an independent working-class political party. Ford obviously was trying to give the party the widest possible appeal to elements of the Negro community and to link their concerns with Soviet foreign policy. This fitted in well with the new United Front strategy.

The party's influence was evidenced by the naming of Davis as executive secretary of the new National Negro Congress and by the adoption of a resolution calling for the expansion of the "Negro United Front" through the congress. The party had campaigned for establishment of the congress during most of 1935 and after it was organized boasted that the action validated the United Front strategy. Now, the Communists thought, many NAACP members could be wooed away and the local branches could be more readily approached. But the Communists could scarcely have been more mistaken.

For the Association as a whole continued to have misgivings, looking askance at some of the delegates at the NNC's first convention. Religious spokesmen who were sympathetic with NAACP aims and had endorsed the gathering were disturbed by the relegation of church delegates to minor roles and the prominent places given to Communists. Negro newspapers were divided on the NNC; some praised it, but the *Chicago Defender* regarded it as an enterprise engineered by the party and likely to pass under Communist control. There was abundant evidence in the NNC's initial operations that if the Communists were not completely in the driver's seat, they were at least mapping the course.[9]

Although Communists and some non-Communists worked diligently to expand the NNC during the first year, the results were disappointing. In Washington a national headquarters was established, and in some of the larger urban centers local councils were formed. Support came primarily from those CIO unions in which the Communists had their greatest influence. The NNC learned with surprise that Negro organizations clutched their purse strings tightly, reluctant to part with funds except for their own specific purposes. Although by 1937, when the second NNC convened, some NAACP leaders had been persuaded to participate, they were at pains to point out that theirs was a personal gesture rather than an organization endorsement; and they came bearing no financial gifts.

[9] A. Philip Randolph, "A. Philip Randolph Tells Why I Would Not Stand for Re-election as President of the National Negro Congress," *American Federationist*, XLVII (July, 1940), 24.

The party's "broad unity" of Negro organizations never came off, in the NNC or elsewhere.

The NNC's prospects were somewhat narrowed by 1937; there were more delegates, but they represented fewer organizations. The Communists, however, were gratified by the fact that Walter White, the NAACP's executive secretary, appeared as a speaker, along with Philip Murray, Thomas Kennedy of the United Mine Workers, Frank Crosswaith of the Harlem Labor Committee, and Norman Thomas of the Socialist Party. The 1937 bent of the NNC was definitely toward labor and political action, while its religious, fraternal, business, and civic group objectives were pushed into the background.

During the next year the NNC was able to secure some cooperation with the NAACP at the branch level while attracting some non-Communist Negro intellectuals who viewed the Association as too slow-moving. The NAACP nationally, however, kept the congress at arm's length. Party influence in the NNC appeared to be growing, with even more of its financial support coming from the Communist-infiltrated unions and front organizations. Where local NAACP branches did undertake joint activities with the NNC there was a tendency for the latter to try to dominate the program. Although under orders to handle the NAACP and its spokesmen carefully, party activists in the NNC were prone to attack them if their cooperation was not unstinting or if they displayed reluctance to participate in the "broad Negro People's Movement." Coupled with this were criticisms of the Association for lacking "progressive," vigorous, and "imaginative" leadership. Confirming the NAACP's worst fears was the fact that in 1938 and 1939 the NNC was not convened, the party reportedly fearing that its grip might be fully exposed and openly challenged. By 1940, when the third convention was held, the party line had changed from United Front to class war again, and with the aid of white pro-Communist union delegates, it forced out Randolph, who had served as NNC president since 1936, as well as other non-Communists, thus capturing the NNC completely; soon the congress became another instrument for the new "anti-imperialist war" line.[10]

Operating through the NNC, the Communists in 1937 were a salient force in forming the Southern Negro Youth Congress (SNYC), which convened in Richmond. Receiving considerable backing from student and other branches of the NAACP, as well as from non-Communist educators, ministers, and labor leaders, the SNYC claimed to represent southern Negro youth. Involvement of the Association's youth chapters was a result of several factors: (1) college communities generally were more receptive to liberal and radical ideas, as both students and faculties were more intensely aware of their own and the race's grievances; (2) faculty sponsors, though mostly non-Communist, had a sharp sensitivity about the critical situation confronting young Negroes and were eager to have them use their learning to racial advantage; (3) student branches chafed under the restraints imposed upon them by the national office; and (4) the national office, having placed little emphasis on youth work, had never developed an imaginative program for channeling student unrest. The conflict between the elders and the angry young men continued, and the Communists made a point of placing young functionaries on colored campuses.

The SNYC stepped into a vacuum. Because of that, many colored educators, politically conservative but racially radical, gave their support to the new congress in spite of certain

---

[10] *Resolutions of the Third National Negro Congress* (Washington, D.C., April, 1940), pp. 4–5; Louis Rosser, testimony, House Committee on Un-American Activities, *Investigation of Communist Activities in the San Francisco Area* (Part I), Dec. 1, 1953, 83rd Cong., 1st sess.; quoted in *Amer. Negro in CP*, pp. 8–9.

risks. Southern Negro ministers of liberal persuasion saw in the SNYC a means of translating the religious idealism of colored youth into practical programs. The fact that both educators and churchmen who endorsed the SNYC were usually identified with the NAACP gave the SNYC some semblance of Association support. Of course, that could but enhance the misgivings of national NAACP leaders.

In not developing its own youth program the NAACP had let pass an opportunity which, if grasped, might have paid off handsomely in the long run, if not immediately. The younger Negro's disillusionment with, or, more aptly, his indifference to, the NAACP might have been countered by a demonstration that the Association did not regard youth work as something peripheral and the youth branches as wards, so to speak, of the regular units. The NAACP might have succeeded in firing the imaginations of Negro youngsters who were receptive to new ideas and eager for things to do in racial protest. It might not have lost to the Communists and other organizations some promising young Negro intellectuals whom it sorely needed.[11] In this connection, it is significant that the virile youth movements of the South in the 1950's and 1960's developed outside rather than inside the NAACP.

True, the Association would have run the risk of having its youth branches captured by the CP or the Young Communist League, on the one hand, or of alienating some of the more conservative and unimaginative leaders of its regular local branches in the South, on the other. It might have been embarrassed by the militancy and brashness of some of the student organizations and by their ineptness in dealing with specific issues or public opinion. However, were the risks not worth taking for such high stakes?

The SNYC's program bore few outward marks of party influence at the time, since the stated objectives of the congress

[11] Interview, anonymous, San Francisco, Calif., Sept. 11, 1957.

closely resembled those embraced by many liberal groups of
the era; in fact, the proposals coincided to a large extent with
what the NAACP had long advocated—an end to lynching, repeal of the poll tax, enfranchisement for Negroes, equality
before the law, economic opportunity and security for colored youth, the right of southern labor to organize (with full
admission of Negroes to unions), modification of the share-
cropper system, and more federal aid to Negro youth through
public works and the schools.[12]

The SNYC's membership, however, was made up primarily
of the better-educated urban Negroes, many of whom would
eventually migrate from the South. Its more knowledgeable
and articulate leaders were drawn from the colleges and universities; they had had little chance for association with their
lower-strata fellows in the industrial or agricultural worlds,
and the social and psychological gaps were difficult to bridge.
Nevertheless, the SNYC did succeed in establishing a headquarters at Richmond (later moved to Birmingham) and in
forming a number of local youth councils in urban centers.
The difficulties it encountered could have been foretold by
the NAACP, which through the years had learned to appreci-
ate the risks of organizing Negro protest, adult or youth, in
the South. Consequently in time the enthusiasm of the 1937
delegates was dampened. Although they were exhilarated by
the first call to action, their ardor cooled rather quickly when
they confronted the mundane tasks of applying the broad
Richmond resolutions in their local communities. The dwindling of interest among the liberal idealists made it easier for
the hard-working, pragmatic Communists to assume direction
of the SNYC's activities and eventually to gain control of the
organization. That trend was climaxed in the party's steering
the SNYC toward opposition to American foreign policy after
the Stalin-Hitler pact in 1939. That the Communist grip was

[12] Editorial, *New Masses*, XXXI (May 10, 1939), 6.

sure was evidenced in the SNYC's docile shifts, in rhythm with the party line, during the war and in the postwar period.[13] Its decreasing appeal for moderate Negro youth was reflected in increased dependency for funds on party-controlled unions.

Another group to make an appearance on the southern scene during the United Front period was the Southern Conference for Human Welfare (SCHW). The NAACP was not prominent in its organization; however, representatives from the Association's southern branches participated in the proceedings of the founding assembly at Birmingham in 1938. In line with its United Front program the Communist Party encouraged formation of the SCHW and eventually dominated it. The conference was a loose grouping of liberal, labor, and Negro forces in the South, who came together for the first time to pursue a program of economic and political action. Inspired initially by the National Emergency Council's shocking *Report on Economic Conditions of the South* (1938), the participants hoped they could find some common ground for social action. The SCHW was a belated and somewhat halting expression of the unrest and reformism which swept the country as submerged and disadvantaged groups raised their political voices. The very fact that it could bring whites and Negroes together for a common effort on regional problems was testimony to the critical and receptive moods of significant segments of the southern populace. Inclusion of such a wide range of interest groups frustrated the attempt of reactionaries to dismiss the SCHW as a Red plot.

The NAACP gave its support to the SCHW but was not entirely at home in it. Although at the top the SCHW was an interracial organization, some of the participating agencies, such as the AFL affiliates, were racially exclusive. Even the CIO had been forced to moderate its demands for Negro rights, as a condition for effective organization in many southern com-

[13] Bunche, *op. cit.*, quoted in Myrdal, *op. cit.*, pp. 818–819.

munities. The SCHW, of course, went on record against lynching and the poll tax, but it was not prepared to challenge the basic patterns of segregation. Had it chosen that course, it might have disintegrated internally immediately and it almost certainly would have encountered such stiff outside opposition as to make its life expectancy short indeed.[14]

Although the ultimate aims of the NAACP—for example, school integration—were not fully incorporated in the SCHW's goals, the Association welcomed the formation of the conference, realizing that even limited measures would, if realized, be of substantial benefit to Negroes, particularly in the economic sphere. Whereas Negroes were allowed some voice in the councils, the SCHW was definitely white-controlled, and the paleskins were disposed to give priority to broad regional needs as they defined them rather than to focus specifically on racial equality. True, Negroes suffered disproportionately in the South from economic, political, and educational handicaps and would therefore have benefited most from an adoption of the SCHW's proposals, provided these were legislated and administered on a nondiscriminatory basis. However, when some of the measures were actually put into effect, colored beneficiaries were few. A strong NAACP in the South could have pressured the SCHW to support more vigorous programs and policed their administration where Negroes were concerned.

Understandably the Association was more willing to support the SCHW than it was to support the NNC or the SNYC. Although the conference included some Communists, white liberals whom the Association regarded as friends predominated. Party functionaries initially were submerged in the SCHW, and the NAACP believed that they could be kept in line, or eliminated if they became too obnoxious. As it turned out,

[14] Charles S. Johnson, "More Southerners Discover the South," *Crisis*, XLI (Jan., 1939), 14–15.

the NAACP was mistaken, but in the beginning it could not afford to be standoffish. The formation of the SCHW posed a perennial issue for the NAACP. Did it dare not go along with any group that promised to alleviate the desperate plight of Negroes? Did it dare go along if the Communists were likely to gain control and subvert the group to their own interests, which might change overnight, leaving the NAACP behind to try to pick up the pieces?

The Communists did not make themselves conspicuous in the early months of the SCHW by voicing demands other than those advocated by liberal-labor groups. Significantly, they did not, as was expected, press the race issue. Like the non-Communist representatives, the Stalinists tended to subsume racial needs in the framework of the SCHW's broad regional program, which was primarily economic in character. They believed that that was the best immediate means of developing Negro-white cooperation in the southern trade-union and political arenas. So concerned was the party with the building of a broad United Front organization in the South that it no doubt would have acquiesced in an even milder racial-rights declaration by the SCHW. Negroes, on the other hand, could but be moved by the SCHW program, limited as it was, since it was one of the first endeavors since the Reconstruction to bring Negroes and whites together on a common program of action outside the framework built by Henry Grady and Booker T. Washington.

Had the NAACP been stronger in the South at the time and participated more extensively in the SCHW, conceivably it could have joined forces with the non-Communist elements in the labor, religious, welfare, and educational groups to keep the conference on its initial course. Over time, with the enthusiasm of many of the participating organizations waning and their activities refocused on national and international issues, the party was able to capture the SCHW, although not without a serious struggle. The SCHW did not have all or even most of the answers to the Negro's problem in the South, and the NAACP leaders knew it. Had they thought otherwise, their support might have been more vigorous.

The NNC, the SNYC, and the SCHW, then, were the principal United Front organizations in which the party sought to build a following among Negroes. The NAACP could scarcely ignore them, but it was ill-equipped to challenge effectively the influence wielded by the Communists. In none of the new agencies could it prevent the Stalinists from eventually gaining control. That did not mean, however, that the Association had stood still. On the contrary, during the United Front period the NAACP overcame some of the conceptual handicaps which hampered it during the early New Deal period.

In the economic sphere it was able to work out profitable relations with the labor movement, especially the CIO wing. In the political arena it began to demonstrate a capacity for agitating and organizing Negro voters. Learning how crucial was the role of government in Negro welfare, it developed further its capacities as a pressure group in both the legislative and administrative areas. Coming out of its relative isolation, it formed alliances with ameliorative groups on such issues as civil rights, education, social welfare, agriculture, and labor. Its concern with foreign affairs was quickened, especially after the rise of Hitler, although, as before, such issues tended to remain secondary in the thinking of its leaders and members. It did not neglect, of course, its primary commitment to the advancement of Negro rights through court processes, and it was during that period that the groundwork was laid for eventual nullification of many of the measures developed by the white South to keep the Negro in his place.

The NAACP's organizational structure remained much the same, and it had little in the way of membership growth to show for its efforts. Some new blood was injected into the official hierarchy; younger publicists, attorneys, and organizers had been added to the staff. The Executive Board was broadened to accommodate a wider range of views and racial interests, reflecting the somewhat altered membership base. In competition with the Communists and their front organizations, the Association suffered some immediate defeats, and it lost to the CP, at least temporarily, the initiative in the propaganda and ideological areas. To them it also lost a number of young colored intellectuals who continued to view the NAACP as too slow-moving and unimaginative.

The conflicting tendencies within the NAACP's national office and Board of Directors were reduced but not resolved. There is a tendency for one social group to view another as a monolithic organization, united against its opponents. Labor had so viewed management, and the white community had so viewed Negroes. The concept was refuted by philosophical differences within the NAACP. Du Bois, for example, had urged Negroes to exploit economically the fact of racial segregation —Negroes should buy from Negro stores, patronize Negro dentists, and so on—although he embraced full integration as an ultimate goal. In that respect he was no different from socialist-minded trade-unionists who compromised doctrinal purity for short-term gains and organizational growth. But in such circumstances it is frequently the radical who is captured by the organization, not the organization that is captured by the radical.[15] That a similar outcome was implicit in Du Bois' pragmatism was recognized by many of the NAACP leaders. James Weldon Johnson, Walter White, and J. E. Spingarn, to mention three, feared that any formal, overt concession to segregated racial patterns would be fatal in the long run, although they recognized that some short-term compromises might be necessary. Particularly did they fear that the mass of Negroes might interpret racial chauvinism

[15] Lawrence, *op. cit.*, p. 97.

as acceptance of segregation on a permanent basis, diluting the ultimate aim of racial equality. They knew that once some concessions were made, the way would be opened for others. Finally, they feared that through short-term gains, some Negroes would acquire a greater vested interest in the segregated system and would therefore be less eager to challenge the biracial pattern.

James Weldon Johnson in his book, *Negro Americans, What Now?* insisted that in spite of the setbacks suffered by Negroes in the early depression period and the temptation to respond in terms of racial separatism and racial nationalism, the NAACP's long-range approach was the only valid one. However, he recognized the importance of the organization's broadening its activities so as to work on race issues with means more direct and more immediately rewarding than legal maneuvers. Knowing as few others did the grip of racism on Negroes as well as whites, he saw little chance that the program of the Communists offered a way out. He held that an acceptance of their approach could only alienate Negroes further from the mainstream of American life, widening the gap between them and those whites who were sensitive to the Negro's plight but willing to better it only within the framework of the existing economic and political order.

Negroes, he argued, could secure jobs without overthrowing capitalism or without establishing a racial economy of their own; Negroes could secure the franchise without discarding the democratic political forms, however ineffectual they might be at the moment. Acceptance of an alien Communist ideology, he insisted, was contrary to the interests not only of whites but of Negroes as well; after all, Negroes drew much of their protest inspiration from the democratic heritage. On the other hand, the separatism proposed by Du Bois, if only as a temporary expedient, offered no real way out, as the failure of all such attempts in the past clearly indicated.

Further, he said, in accepting either of those extremes the
NAACP would forfeit the possibility of appealing to the white
man's conscience and sense of guilt, for Negroes themselves
would be rejecting the basic moral premises out of which
that conscience and guilt grew.[16]

Spingarn's position was medial but somewhat closer to that
of Du Bois. The idea, for example, that Negroes might be
able to employ their consumer power to press for jobs in
retail establishments or to form Negro cooperatives appealed
to Spingarn. The national office had supported with little enthusiasm those local branches engaged in such campaigns. In
some of the large urban centers of the North the slogan, "Don't
Buy Where You Can't Work," caught hold to the extent
that the NAACP and the CP fell into line with it, although both
organizations insisted officially that that approach offered no
final solution even for the economic aspects of the race problem.[17]

Du Bois had no particular sympathy with the party; he
fought it through *Crisis* and other publications until he resigned in 1934. Only after leaving the NAACP did he become
enthusiastic about some of the causes and organizations, such
as the SNYC, that carried the Communist blessing. In the showdown with White and Spingarn, Du Bois' position on the
party was not an issue; the differences were to a large extent
personal, centering on the amount of freedom accorded the
Crisis editor. The low and poorly concealed opinions that
Du Bois held of some of the national staff and Executive
Board members were contributing factors, aggravating more
basic disagreements. As a first-rate intellectual and an "en-
thusiast" within the organization, Du Bois felt that he was
being forced increasingly into a bureaucratic mold from which
resignation was the only escape. He departed the NAACP in

[16] New York: Viking Press, 1934, *passim*.
[17] Lawrence, *op. cit.*, p. 287.

July, 1934, resisting the efforts of the national staff and the Board to work out a reconciliation. Perhaps to his surprise the man who had been editor of *Crisis*, director of research, and one of the founding fathers learned that his departure was not fatal to the organization.

When James Weldon Johnson had left the NAACP in 1931, Walter White had become the executive secretary. Less doctrinaire and also less intellectually sophisticated than Du Bois, White, who was to become the symbol of the NAACP during the next two decades, broadened greatly the NAACP's contacts with other organizations at a time when the opportunity to do so was greatest. White was a social sophisticate and had great facility in public relations plus a flair for popular writing, public speaking, and the creation of a favorable public image of the organization among both Negroes and whites. An inveterate name-dropper, he really knew and was liked by hundreds of celebrities in café society, among the literati, in the political sphere, in sports, and in other fields. He was no stranger at the White House.[18] Often impatient with ideological and intellectual questions, he extended more or less openhanded acceptance to those who, for whatever motives, would support the NAACP's program. Coupled with other frailties were a certain shortsightedness, an often unwarranted optimism, and an inability to scrutinize as critically as had Johnson (and, later, Roy Wilkins) the party's overtures to the Association. His soft handling of the Communists during his early years as NAACP secretary was not a consequence of any sympathy for their aims or methods, but rather a failure to understand fully the nature of the movement and to see its long-term implications.

In that, of course, he was not alone; after all, the middle 1930's was the heyday of party respectability. But White

[18] Lillian Smith, "Negroes in Grey Flannel Suits," *Progressive*, XX (Feb., 1956), p. 35.

eventually learned—the hard way—that similarity of slogans did not necessarily signify agreement on means, not to mention ultimate ends. Even so, the meaning of Scottsboro and the ILD's role in that tragic episode he may never have fully comprehended. Biographers of Walter White will one day have to gauge his failures as well as his achievements, and in assessing the former it will be difficult to avoid the conclusion that, although he had public relations and organizational savvy, he lacked intellectual depth and political sophistication. It is not surprising that he never really understood Du Bois. What is striking is the fact that they could remain under the same organizational roof and work together for so long. All this, however, is not to underestimate White's crucial contributions to the NAACP or his dedication to it.

The NAACP's staff and Executive Board members were to learn a great deal from and about the party during the United Front period and to forget very little. They insisted on maintaining the Association's autonomy when in effect the Stalinists were insisting that its identity be lost in a "Negro People's movement." Seeing the possibilities of appealing to lower-strata Negroes at the economic level, Association leaders reshaped their program to include such issues as relief, public employment, and organization of labor, knowing that indifference to or failure in those areas might enable the Communists to win by default. The 1930's were a period when indigenous dissent groups in the United States increasingly came to view the state as an instrument of social reform; even the labor movement, which had been almost syndicalist in its voluntarism, began to embrace political action. The NAACP rowed in the mainstream, attempting to gain the ear of government for the Negro's interests and to give the Negro a voice in government through extension of the franchise. Indeed, the NAACP stressed to Negroes the idea that government could be used to realize racial aims; certainly the state was not a hostile class enemy to be by-passed and later over-thrown.

Admittedly the NAACP failed to reach the mass of Negroes in the rural South or to do much about their condition; but in the urban North for the first time it established contacts with groups other than the black *bourgeoisie* and the Talented Tenth. To that end it was forced to take serious cognizance of radical ideologies and movements which previously it had regarded as irritants or as extremist flurries. In dealing with leftist movements some of its already limited energies were diverted from more immediate racial concerns, but one result was increased political sophistication and new organizational techniques which eventually were turned to good account. Competing with the Communists, nationalists, jackleg preachers, and simple Machiavellians, the NAACP's leaders all along the line were forced to clarify for themselves, as well as for others, their ideas and goals in the context of crisis.

In doing so they laid at least the groundwork for appeals to some of the young Negro intellectuals who in the following two decades were to sharpen and invigorate the Association. Communists and Communist sympathizers among Negroes, increasingly disillusioned with the party even during the peak of the United Front period, began to entertain some hope that the NAACP might develop into something that was intellectually challenging and organizationally rewarding. To those who retained their Stalinist identities the NAACP presented increasingly effective challenges. Its national staff members and branch officers acquired, along with bitter experience, a new comprehension of how "true believers" actually operate. From the admittedly advantageous perspective of more than two decades, what impresses one about the Association during the United Front period is not how much it was directly influenced and used by the CP, but how little.

If there remained any doubts about the Communist Party's

attachment to the Kremlin and the Third International or
any illusions concerning its claim to be the spokesman of the
Negro people, they were quickly destroyed following the
signing of the Stalin-Hitler pact in August, 1939. The new
line of the party called for all-out opposition to the allied
powers and for noninvolvement of the United States in international collective security programs, whatever the price. The
Communists turned on Roosevelt with a venom surpassing
that of the early New Deal period and dropped their effort
to form united fronts with political, labor, and racial movements. Courting its old enemies—the isolationist *Chicago
Tribune*, the America Firsters, the Coughlinites, and the German Bundists—the party turned its back on groups that did
not fall in behind its slogan of "Keep America Out of the
Imperialist War." Since the details of this spectacle have been
reported at great length in other studies, there is little need
to recount them here; the present concern is with the meaning of the shift for relations between the NAACP and the
CP during the period from August, 1939, to June, 1941.[19]

During the United Front period the party had made numerous bids for cooperation with the moderate Negro organizations, as has been described. Through the National
Negro Congress the Stalinists had tried to give the United
Front program its fullest expression among Negroes. In that
they had achieved a measure of success but not nearly what
they had hoped to realize. Whether or not the NNC could
eventually have been shaped into a more effective instrument
had the United Front line remained in force is a matter of
conjecture. It seems clear that even before the Stalin-Hitler
agreement the congress showed weaknesses which could but
lead to its demise or at most to its continuation as another
isolated collection of the party faithful. By 1938 the high hopes
that non-Communists such as Ralph Bunche had originally

[19] W. Record, *op. cit.*, pp. 247–253.

held for the NNC were fading rapidly in view of its failure to do much more than issue pronouncements and carry out limited propaganda endeavors. Although active as a lobbying organization in the nation's capital and able to form a number of local councils, it failed to enlist many Negro organizations in concrete cooperative programs or to generate the grassroots racial upsurge which had been its principal objective.

With the Nazis and Communists coming to terms in Europe, the CP in the United States quickly tempered its anti-Fascist mien. Further, its vociferous internationalism was transmuted into equally vociferous isolationism. Every organization it controlled swung into action against Roosevelt's quasi-interventionist foreign policy. At the same time it suddenly fawned upon groups it had previously declared to be mortal foes. Indeed, the party was now willing to destroy any organization that it could not bend to isolationism. Where full control could not be gained, as in many of the unions in which it had some strength, the party tried to create internal dissension on foreign policy issues and to hamper the defense effort in key industries by political strikes, demonstrations, slowdowns, and less direct means.[20] In short, for the Stalinists the sole criterion for judging an organization had become its position on foreign policy. Thus the German-American Bund and the *Chicago Tribune* rose in favor while the NAACP and the *New York Times* were abused daily.

The Association had continuously voiced its opposition to fascism, whose racial philosophies, particularly in Germany, were abhorrent. Such attraction as the party had for some of the NAACP members during the United Front period was predicated in part on the presumed anti-Nazism of the USSR and the CPUSA. However, foreign policy and European ideologies were not the principal concern of Negroes or the NAACP.

[20] Max M. Kampelman, *The Communist Party vs the CIO* (New York: Praeger, 1957), p. 57.

The issue of internationalism versus isolationism was low on the Negro's agenda. Although there was some sensitivity to events affecting colonial peoples, it remained largely unfocused in the face of persistent domestic problems. The NAACP had displayed an awakening concern (in part the result of Du Bois' influence) about imperialist subjugation of the natives of Asia and Africa. However, that issue was not the Association's controlling standard for judging a person's or an organization's worth.

In a very real sense the NAACP was neither interventionist nor isolationist; it was pro-Negro. While its leaders were anti-Hitler, they were quite aware that neither Britain nor France could claim to be a paragon in its relations with colored peoples. So the NAACP found it hard to become enthusiastic about the British Empire even if it was fighting Hitler. The Association needed no reminder that the Negro had fought for democracy before, only to be rewarded with continued discrimination.

In 1939 there was considerable antiwar sentiment among Negroes, a mood that the Communists attempted to capitalize. But the feeling was vague; it could not be organized. Invoking images of imperialist Britain and France, reviving Negro memories of the post-World War I era, and appealing to quasi-pacifist sentiments, the Communists sought to discredit the NAACP, which it accused of being prowar and interventionist. In particular, the party was critical of Walter White, Roy Wilkins, J. E. Spingarn, and A. Philip Randolph. Not that they campaigned actively for American preparedness and intervention; it was enough to condemn them in party eyes that they refused to place the Association squarely in opposition to any defense or allied-aid program.

While the Communists were attempting to exploit pacifist sentiments among Negroes and others, something else was happening to keep racial concerns domestically oriented. The

European war and increased defense spending at home brought a general rise in American employment, partially relieving the Negro's foremost economic problem. Along with many others victimized by the depression, Negroes found that war was not an unmixed evil if it brought jobs and a chance to get off relief rolls. Being the most disadvantaged group in the labor force, they would have been loath to forgo the new job possibilities even if they had felt strongly isolationist. Besides, there was the accompanying feeling that major directions in American foreign policy were well beyond their influence anyway, so they might as well make the most of any opportunities which came their way.

The NAACP leaders, of course, were more sophisticated. They could grasp more clearly the implications of a Hitler conquest, not only for Europe but for the Negro in the United States. Although aware of the shortcomings of American democracy, they did not, as did the Communists, attempt to equate Roosevelt's America with Hitler's Germany. Increasingly they came to feel, as did others who during the interwar period had developed pacifist leanings, that America, including Negro America, might have a definite stake in the European hostilities. Unlike Du Bois in World War I, the Association leaders did not issue a ringing call for Negroes to close ranks and give their all to the struggle. Nor did they feel that anything was to be gained by uncompromising opposition. The Communists, for whom the issue was a black-and-white matter, characterized the Association's qualified support of American foreign policy and the defense program as "a sell-out to the warmongers," "treacherous," and "hiding behind the protective coloration of democracy while openly trying to win the Negroes to support of the British-American gang of imperialists as against the Hitler gang." [21]

[21] Benjamin Davis, Jr., review of the pamphlet *Democracy Means Jobs for Negroes*, in *Daily Worker*, May 23, 1941, p. 7

The NAACP suspected that the party would attempt to put the Negro's vague antiwar sentiments and not so vague economic distress to good use. As it turned out, the NAACP and other ameliorative groups beat the party to the draw. In cooperation with the National Urban League, the Brotherhood of Sleeping Car Porters, and other organizations, the Association in 1940 helped to form the March on Washington Movement (MOWM) to demand equitable employment opportunities for Negroes in defense plants and better treatment of colored men called into the services. MOWM leaders, chiefly Randolph, accepted the defense program and military conscription as realities. They did not believe they could influence significantly the decision to get in or stay out of the war. Their main concern was to guard the interests of Negroes whatever came, and they were ready to try a bold stroke—to organize a mass march of Negroes on the capital of the United States. Whether or not they could have succeeded is conjectural; that they were prepared to make the effort there can be no doubt. Only Roosevelt's issuance of Executive Order 8802, establishing the Committee on Fair Employment Practice (FEPC), stayed the command to march.

The Stalinists did not know what to do about the MOWM. They condemned its acceptance of the defense effort and its eagerness to make Negroes a part of the defense production scheme. On the other hand, the party rejoiced at anything which might discredit the Roosevelt administration and could scarcely conceive a more embarrassing spectacle than thousands of Negroes converging upon the President with demands that he do something about their plight. The party had been forced to sit up and take notice at the way Negroes responded to the MOWM. To curry favor with aroused colored people, the Communists endorsed the demand for an end to discrimination in defense jobs but insisted in the same breath that the whole defense program be abandoned.

The Communists could neither destroy nor capture the MOWM, since Randolph had taken precautions against their infiltration, specifically excluding them from the organization.[22] In this he was aided by Walter White and other tacticians in the NAACP's national office. Randolph had learned a great deal about Communist methods in his long tenure as president of the Brotherhood of Sleeping Car Porters and as president for four years of the National Negro Congress. In the latter office he had observed how party functionaries moved into controlling positions and finally threw him out when he opposed their efforts to convert the congress into an "anti-imperialist war" apparatus at the expense of Negro interests. In him the Stalinists had found a formidable adversary, personal and philosophical.

In aligning itself with the MOWM, the NAACP pitted its strength squarely against the Communists. The Association energetically drove home to Negroes the charge that the CP was not primarily interested in either the Negro or peace, though it talked a lot about both. NAACP leaders highlighted the fact that the party's concern for Negro workers and share-croppers was a sometime thing, subject to immediate abandonment on signal from the Kremlin. Evidence that the party was willing to destroy organizations such as the NNC, SNYC, and SCHW, if such action served its purposes, was publicized for all to see.[23]

By challenging segregation in the defense plants and armed services, without isolating itself or Negroes from the main currents of American life, the NAACP struck a responsive chord; the program redounded to its benefit during the war and post-

[22] A. Philip Randolph, "March on Washington Movement Offers Program," in Rayford Logan, ed., *What the Negro Wants* (Chapel Hill: University of North Carolina Press, 1944), pp. 148–149.

[23] George S. Schuyler, "Have Communists Stopped Fighting for Negro Rights?" *Negro Digest*, III (Dec., 1944), 63–64.

war periods. The Association's firmly based position contrasted markedly with that of the party, which had suffered serious organizational and ideological damage among Negroes. By refraining from the use of racial grievances to undermine American policies during an emergency period, the Association improved its bargaining position with the American public. Emphasizing that its goals, if realized, would make the nation stronger at home and abroad, the Association was gratified to see those goals begin to be incorporated in the defense effort. Its moral and ideological position was virtually unassailable; it was asking for nothing more than validation of the very ethical principles which America was presumably girding to defend. With telling vigor the NAACP pointed out that the treatment of Negroes in the United States would have an important bearing on the responses of colored peoples over the world whom the allied nations were attempting to win to their cause. Unlike the Communists, it could pressure Roosevelt without having to break with him, and that was important because he had become a symbol of hope for many Negroes. Of course, the gains won by Negroes during the war were not handed them on a silver salver—they had to be fought for. After all, Roosevelt set up the FEPC only after Negroes threatened to march on Washington.

Because the Association championed Negro industrial workers and servicemen, its membership, particularly in the urban industrial centers, soared to 400,000 by 1946. To make its demands more acceptable to whites, it reminded them of the loyalty of Negroes in the past, despite segregation and mistreatment.

In contrast, the CP's colored membership, never large, was drastically reduced and could not be replenished. While the NAACP and the march on Washington received wide acclaim and strong editorial support, the Negro press became increasingly hostile toward Communists. The party had been able to navigate in the broad stream of American liberalism during the United Front period; now it was fighting the current, and few Negroes were willing to paddle at its side. Even when the party took up specific Negro grievances, it was handicapped by the necessity of tying racial protest to "getting out and staying out of the imperialist war." For many Negroes who for years had been unemployed and on relief rolls and who now had jobs, the war was something less than a catastrophe, as it was also for whites in the same condition.

In unions Negro workers were more concerned about wages and promotions than about foreign policy issues; the party's preoccupation with nonunion matters and its willingness to compromise bread-and-butter issues for political advantage only enhanced the growing skepticism of black laborers, whose friends the Stalinists claimed to be. Politically, Negroes remained loyal to Roosevelt, giving him a thumping majority of their votes in 1940; the NAACP and the MOWM, in spite of their criticism of some of his policies, had a decided hand in the result. In contrast, the Communists not only attacked F.D.R. as, among other things, anti-Negro; they even lambasted Mrs. Roosevelt, and to the American Negro that was truly going too far. The President's wife had become a patron saint to underprivileged Americans. Langston Hughes's famous Harlem character, Simple, once mused that he hoped God would "smite white folks down" at the Second Coming. When asked if he meant all white folks, Simple replied, "No, I hope he lets Mrs. Roosevelt alone."

When the Germans attacked Russia in June, 1941, the CP in the United States, again taking its cues from the Kremlin, executed another somersault. Like the performance of August, 1939, the 1941 head-over-heels has been extensively documented, and there is no need to review the details here.[24] The present concern is this: How did the new line affect NAACP-CP

24 W. Record, op. cit., pp. 183–186.

117

relations? Recall the party's over-all program during the preceding two years. Its major objective had been to hamstring American defense, conscription, and foreign aid. To that end it had called political strikes, urged Negroes to oppose the defense effort, and evidenced willingness to collaborate with groups ranging the political spectrum, the only requirement being opposition to the "imperialist war."

By August, 1941, however, the Stalinists were employing their trade-union influence to increase production of war materials, imploring Negroes not to press racial demands, organizing intellectuals as prowar propagandists, and seeking to reestablish themselves with those groups—political, labor, and racial—which they had roundly denounced in the 1939–1941 interlude. Almost overnight Communists changed from vocal opponents of an imperialist war to outspoken supporters of a war for national liberation.[25]

Did that mean that the CP would once again attempt *rapprochement* with the NAACP, which it had so recently characterized as a "traitor to the Negro People" and a "collaborator of the warmongers"? Hardly. The NAACP now had a two-pronged aim: (1) advancement of the rights of the Negro and (2) defeat of the Fascists. During the 1939 to 1941 period the Communists urged the sacrifice of (2) for (1); now it wanted to sacrifice (1) for (2). Accordingly, the Communists continued to denounce the NAACP and its leaders, but for quite different reasons. With the NAACP's continuing insistence that (1) and (2) were not contradictory objectives, the Communists stepped up their attacks on its leaders and went so far as to insist that they were saboteurs, traitors, and subversives. The party did not stoop to public demands that White, Wilkins, Gloster Current, Spingarn, and other NAACP leaders be jailed;

[25] James W. Ford, "Some Problems of the Negro People in the National Front to Destroy Hitler and Hitlerism," *Communist*, XX (Oct., 1941), 888–896.

it is not rash to conjecture, however, that no defense funds would have been raised by the party in their behalf had such a fate befallen them. To the Communists anything that rocked the production boat or could possibly delay aid to the USSR smacked of sedition.

The *volte-face* of the Communists underscored again their Comintern ties, as it did their opportunistic approach to Negro rights. Although the NAACP leaders already knew the party's nature, they did not quite anticipate the extent to which it would go: a prompt surrender of all its racial, worker, and political programs to become the ally of racists, reactionary employers, and the lunatic political fringe.

The *Daily Worker* proclaimed that

the Negro people can now be found among the first to recognize the changed character of the European conflict since the invasion of the Soviet Union, and will see the world-wide dangers inherent in Hitler's attack upon the stronghold of racial equality and freedom.[26]

Wrapping himself in both banners—Stars and Stripes as well as Hammer and Sickle—James W. Ford declared that "the struggle for the rights of the Negro people is an inescapable part of the struggle . . . of the international people's front to defeat and destroy Hitler fascism." The Negro conservative, Dr. Gordon Hancock, was "absolutely right," Ford continued, when the professor told his audience, "Negroes, this is our war." [27] Ford neglected to mention that Dr. Hancock had been saying that in 1940, too.

Such declarations gave witness to the CP's readiness to give Negro war support away free instead of using it as a bargaining lever for racial rights. Not so the NAACP, which insisted that Negroes be given equal responsibilities and advantages as

[26] July 15, 1941, p. 6.
[27] "Some Problems of the Negro People."

well as equal sacrifices. Ford claimed to discern in the Association a shift in orientation toward unqualified endorsement of the war production, conscription, and foreign aid programs, but that was certainly not the case; or if it was, the CP's and the NAACP's conceptions of "full support" were horses of disparate color.

The CP claimed that it, too, had been concerned about Negro rights in the industrial and military areas all along and that Hitler's attack on Russia had led only to a shift in emphasis. Its protestations fell on jaded ears. While the CP now proclaimed that the fullest utilization of manpower necessitated the elimination of discriminatory patterns in industry and the armed services, it did little more than mouth the slogans; any attempt to implement them found the party trying to put a damper on dissent.

Only in the very late stages of the war, when the CP concluded that pressures for racial rights enhanced industrial and military efficiency and when its loss of Negro support was almost complete, did it make a few gestures toward an antidiscrimination program.[28] For most of the war its main activity was to stifle Negro protest and to urge black workers and soldiers to get into line on the white man's terms, just as it urged unions to get on with the production job, on the bosses' terms if necessary. Even the Stalinists themselves admitted this following the close of the conflict.[29]

Draping itself in the flag and proclaiming its 200 per cent Americanism, the CP used its resources to try to keep the lid on labor and Negro unrest; it denounced as "betrayers" and "traitors" those union and racial leaders who dared to pull a strike or a slowdown or to withhold full sanction of any war production task, no matter what the task entailed in indignity

---

[28] Lawrence, *op. cit.*, p. 634.

[29] James W. Ford, "Revisionist Policies Weakened Struggles for Negro Rights," *Daily Worker*, June 25, 1945, p. 7.

or hardship. That Negroes might demand, as a price for fighting on battlefields or speeding up production on war jobs, some concrete demonstration that the democracy they were called upon to defend against foreign enemies would be validated in the Negro community at home was unthinkable for the Communist. For to the dedicated party member, the ultimate hope of humanity, black or brown or white, lies in the triumph of communism, and to that end every other consideration must be subjugated. The Communist reasoning is simple: the Negro can never achieve full rights under capitalism, which is inherently exploitive and oppressive; only under communism can the black man—and the rest of humanity—be truly free; Russia, the Communist fatherland, was fighting for its very survival; it must be saved at all costs so that it could spread communism to the rest of the world; therefore any struggle for Negro rights which might disrupt American production or delay the opening of a second front—and thereby jeopardize the USSR's chances of survival—also put in jeopardy the very Negro rights which shortsighted NAACP leaders were foolish enough to try to pursue at that critical time. It is this rationale which non-Communists must fully understand if they are to comprehend how individual party members who sincerely believed in the dignity of black men and sincerely wanted their liberation could remain faithful to the party through such contortions of policy as occurred in 1939 and 1941. Viewed through party lenses, what appeared to outsiders to be blatantly cynical and unprincipled behavior had an underlying principle after all—and one which could be stated in humanitarian terms.

Paralleling the experience of World War I, the Association's membership increased rapidly during World War II, reaching almost 400,000 toward the close of the conflict. The Association was working diligently, with a limited staff, in behalf of fair employment opportunities for the race in industry. It had been one of the chief organizations that obtained Roosevelt's Executive Order 8802, which prohibited discrimination in war plants and the establishment of the FEPC as an enforcing agency. However, the effectiveness of the order and of the committee depended largely on what Negroes themselves did in bringing complaints and keeping the pressure up. Here the NAACP staff was invaluable. In generating support for the committee and in acting as watchdog on its operations, the NAACP put to good use the skills it had developed in its prewar court cases, especially its franchise suits. It is not sufficient to get laws passed and executive orders issued; somebody has to ferret out the violations and bring them to trial or hearing. For that task local NAACP branches were irreplaceable during the war, as they have been in the postwar school cases.

The War Production Board, the War Labor Board, the War Manpower Commission, and other agencies responsible for organizing the nation's material and manpower resources became acquainted with the NAACP. Through its Washington office it pressed for clauses in wartime legislative measures that would protect the rights of racial minorities; it opposed moves disadvantageous to Negro workers and servicemen. In the urban communities outside the South—and there, too, to some extent—it provided migrant Negroes with one of their few opportunities for forming associational ties about racial concerns; this was reflected in the rapid growth of membership and in a much wider knowledge of the NAACP among Negroes.[30]

Its propaganda work was much expanded; since it was in the forefront of a host of activities which received extensive coverage in the Negro press, it no longer had to depend primarily on its own publications to get its views across. The NAACP was news—big news—even in the general press.

[30] Between 1940 and 1945 the membership of the NAACP increased from 50,556 to 351,131, with the growth in the southeastern region being almost tenfold.

The Association eagerly joined the "Double V" campaign —victory over fascism abroad and victory over discrimination at home—a project launched by leading Negro newspapers which gained momentum throughout the war. Neither the Communist Party nor any of its front organizations in the race field endorsed the movement, though it elicited a large response from Negroes. On the contrary, the party and its agencies branded the campaign as disruptive, apparently fearing, wrongly as it turned out, that it would delay aid to the USSR, especially the opening of a second front.

Although the FEPC was hobbled from the outset because it lacked a legislative base, had only limited funds, and was confronted by opposition from employers and many trade-unions, its accomplishments during the first two years were encouraging to the Negro organizations that had brought it into being. NAACP leaders believed it could do more, but they recognized that the FEPC's chief significance lay not so much in its immediate accomplishments as in its service as a precedent for future policies of the government. Some kind of surveillance of government contracts with respect to racial discrimination was no doubt here to stay.

The FEPC was threatened with extinction in 1943, primarily at the initiative of Paul V. McNutt, then director of the War Manpower Commission. The MOWM and the NAACP rallied quickly to its defense; Randolph and White seriously considered renewing the march on Washington. They certainly received no encouragement from the CP. Indeed, the Stalinists were emphasizing not how little but how much was being done for Negroes by the FEPC and by other government agencies. Some propaganda on the Negro problem was carried in party media, particularly the *Daily Worker*, but there was much more militancy in the *Chicago Defender*.

The party was especially disturbed by the emergence of Randolph not only as a Negro labor leader but as a general race spokesman. The president of the Brotherhood of Sleeping Car Porters had fought and beaten the Communists in his own union; his opposition had hampered party efforts to build Negro followings in both the CIO and AFL. Although he had been involved in some of the United Front race organizations, such as the NNC, he was his own man and displayed a fierce independence which the Stalinists could not breach. But though they feared Randolph might make further inroads on CP influence in the unions and among Negroes generally, they could not completely denounce him without at the same time frontally attacking the MOWM, and this they were reluctant to do after the MOWM successes, lest they alienate many more Negroes. The party had no racial organizations of its own to speak of.[31] The National Negro Congress had been thoroughly discredited; it managed to maintain a few of its local councils and to carry on mild protests here and there, but it was virtually defunct. Randolph's influence grew in the NAACP, a fact reflected in his being awarded the Spingarn Medal in 1942 and later being named a member of the Executive Board. The Communists feared he might go too far in his demands for Negro rights, "isolating the Negro people" from the "win the war camp." [32]

During the war period the Communists talked loudly and carried a twig. They barked and snipped at MOWM heels. The party's effort to infiltrate the MOWM, which was the only feasible tactic in the circumstances, got nowhere, due in large part to Randolph's having anticipated the maneuver and established checks against it. Had the party captured the MOWM, it, like the NNC and the SNYC, would have become a wartime "Uncle Tom" outfit.

A big reason for Communist opposition to the MOWM was

[31] Lawrence, *op. cit.*, p. 376.

[32] James W. Ford, "The Negro People Unite for Victory," *Communist*, XXII (July, 1943), 643.

the latter's success, at least temporarily, in bringing non-Communist Negro organizations such as the NAACP and the NUL into a close working alliance, something that the Communists had failed to do. Moreover, these agencies were getting things done, although accomplishments generally fell short of hopes. The NAACP's autonomy, of course, was in no way compromised by its participation in the MOWM, which was a loose federation; Randolph and the NAACP leaders were astute enough to recognize that joint endeavors could be seriously disrupted if any organization believed its independence was being compromised. The fact that there was considerable overlapping of NAACP and Sleeping Car Porter membership in local communities facilitated the work of the MOWM committees.[33]

Although the MOWM failed to survive the war period, it laid the groundwork for cooperation between Negro organizations and perfected protest techniques which were to be widely copied, for example, the civil rights mobilization strategy followed by the NAACP beginning in 1950.

As the Communists were largely on the sidelines of Negro protest during the war, they could do little more than boo the gladiators on the field. By late 1943 the party's Uncle Tomism had become so transparent that its leaders felt that at least a few gestures should be made toward advancing Negro rights. To that end the Communists used such organizations as the NNC and the SNYC to launch occasional protests against racial discrimination in the military and in industry. Such objections, however, were feeble, and when some party project threatened to develop into strenuous opposition which might even remotely endanger production or military effectiveness, the Stalinists were willing to protest for the record and then hastily call the whole thing off.

[33] For a description of the "occupational culture" of the Sleeping Car Porters and its significance for their involvement in protest and betterment activities, see Brazeal, *op. cit.*

While all this was going on, the NAACP was growing in numbers and influence precisely because it was not afraid to propagandize and pressure for a fair deal for Negroes in industry, military services, civilian defense, and the Red Cross. It was not afraid to risk charges that it was hampering conduct of the war and using national security to bargain for racial goals. It was unwilling to accept a promissory note on Negro rights payable entirely after the end of the emergency; it had held such paper before only to find the value withered after the emergency was over.

Having learned that Negro protest on immediate issues could be the source of organizational strength, it showed no disposition to permit racial unrest to go unchanneled or to risk a later accusation that it had sacrificed rank-and-file interest to bureaucratic timidity and the failure of leadership imagination. Thus emerged a paradox: the NAACP found itself in the somewhat curious position of being a moderate organization behaving in a militant way, while the CP, ostensibly radical—even revolutionary—was, hat in hand, asking white masters what they would have the colored man do to help the war effort.

To give some substance to its belated decision to speak out for Negro rights, though not too loudly, the party launched the Negro Labor Victory Committee (NLVC), centered in New York. The NLVC proclaimed its intention of doing something about discrimination against Negroes in industry and the armed forces; but, whereas it did make some public fuss about a few cases of racial injustice, its main aim was to counter the MOWM and the NAACP, mobilizing Negro labor and other groups behind a second front campaign.[34] Indeed, so small were the results that the NAACP took only slight official cognizance of the NLVC, while watching its frantic maneuvers carefully from the sidelines. The party in the Negro community never recovered from its wartime deser-

[34] *Amer. Negro in CP*, p. 12.

tion of the racial struggle. Communists entertained some doubts about their Uncle Tomism even then, but it was not until the postwar period that they awoke to the fact that they might have permanently dropped the ball. The later self-flagellation of its leaders, especially Negroes such as Winston, Davis, Wilkerson, Ford, and Jones, could not reconstruct the past; the moving finger had writ, and all the self-recrimination in the world could not wash out a word.[35]

With the "dissolution" of the party in May, 1944, Communists thought they would be in a better position to advance the interests of the USSR. As a matter of fact, it was at the behest of the latter that the liquidation was initiated. Later, of course, it was made to appear that the initiative was supplied by the "opportunist" Browder and his followers, who led the Stalinist virgins into "the swamp of revisionism" and there deprived them of their innocence. When it dissolved, the party was "replaced" by the Communist Political Association (CPA), whose outward appearance differed little from the "social-democrat" and "reformist" movements which the Stalinists had denounced for years. It extended its hand to capitalism, which, it said, was capable of gradual reformation; it rejected revolution and the class struggle as a means of social change and an avenue to power; it embraced the desirability of such bourgeois values as a free press, free speech, democratic elections, and an independent judiciary. Rejecting the self-determination doctrine for Negroes, it now visualized a gradual movement toward integration. Negroes, declared the CPA, had long shown their determination to become an integral part of American society; in effect they had already exercised the choice between racial separatism on the one hand and full citizenship in American society on the other.[36]

[35] Herbert Hill, "The Communist Party: Enemy of Negro Equality," *Crisis*, LVIII (June, 1951), 369–370.

[36] Robert Minor, *The Heritage of the Communist Political Association* (New York: International Publishers, 1945), p. 45.

The response of the NAACP to this move was something less than ecstatic. While its leaders did not regret the ostensible self-liquidation of a radical sect that had been the source of many troubles for almost two decades, they were not taken in by the latest Stalinist maneuver, having learned the extent to which Communists would go in furthering their goals and how opportunist their approaches to Negroes were. Relations between the NAACP and the CPA during the brief existence of the latter (May, 1944, to July, 1945) were so limited that they can be dealt with tersely. The dissolution of the CP opened the way for Communists to reapproach the NAACP as a reformist political movement, but the Association was as unreceptive to the CP's successor as it had been to the CP.

By that time the Communists, whether parading under the banner of the CP or the CPA or some front organization, were prisoners of their past. The NAACP's national and branch leaders found it difficult to believe that the leopard had really changed his spots, that lion (or, more appropriately, bear) had been transmuted into lamb. Randolph and White pointed out in 1944 that whatever organizational guise Communists might assume it would be folly for Negroes to link their fate in any way to the party's.[37] Disdaining the CPA at the national level, the NAACP tried to stem its penetration of local branches here and there—in Philadelphia, Chicago, Richmond (California), and Detroit. Significantly, the CPA did not make any effort to liquidate its race organizations—the ILD, NNC, SNYC, NLVC— which Communists had either built outright or captured. This was a tip-off, if one were needed, that the party had no intention of dismantling its action apparatus to become a study association.

Because the NAACP was growing rapidly, its membership reaching an all-time high totaling many times that of a few years earlier, Communist opposition came increasingly to be

[37] Randolph, "March on Washington Movement."

viewed as a buzzing fly rather than as a poised rattler. The NAACP's leaders were confronted with organizational issues of the first magnitude; the multiplication of local branches, increased demands for services from the field, and growth of internal administrative problems claimed an ever larger portion of their energies.

The NAACP's rapid growth was not, from an organizational standpoint, an unmixed blessing. People with little understanding of its goals or methods signed up, expecting almost immediate delivery on their demands and sometimes exhibiting impatience or disillusionment if they were not quickly filled. In local communities politically ambitious Negroes saw in some of the NAACP branches, growing as they were into large organizations, an opportunity to capture a following that might serve personal ambitions. Furthermore, many new members were unsophisticated politically and so much in need of practical leadership that Communist activists moved in. A dozen or more local branches, including one in Richmond, California, which was composed largely of Negro shipyard workers fresh from the South, were captured. The job of educating, guiding, and servicing the many new branches stretched thin the resources of the national staff, and the Association's inability to develop stable local leadership helped produce a high branch mortality during the immediate postwar years. This was especially true in the Pacific and mountain states, to which Negroes were moving in large numbers for the first time.

Not only was the national staff relatively small; much of its time was consumed in working with wartime government agencies to the neglect of local organizational problems. Some NAACP national staff members had entered the armed services; others accepted positions with government agencies; still others became involved with local commissions on human relations established by forward-looking communities to deal with racial tensions and problems. Thus resources which might have been concentrated on the hard day-to-day tasks of building viable branches were scattered. Although Negroes benefited from such outside activities, the NAACP's internal organizational problems proliferated.

NAACP leaders were cognizant of the deficiencies, but there was little they could do. Had they been able to place a hundred, even fifty, capable representatives in the field, the organization would have been much stronger today. The problem of staffing, however, was more than one of money; finding willing personnel capable of organizing Negroes and channeling their protest was difficult. Few able Negroes were willing to make a profession of protest, especially when fresh opportunities beckoned in other directions.

Ironically, the very success of the NAACP in breaking down barriers to education and employment make it increasingly difficult to recruit staff members from talented young Negroes who reap the greatest benefits from its efforts. In order to attract them, the NAACP must tap their idealism and racial pride; it must also hold out to them the image of a better world. The mere goal of getting what white folk have cannot be counted on to inspire them; for some will always ask whether what the white folk have is really worth having. This bit of truth, which became clearer in the 1960's, first presented itself in the war period.

With the close of the war the NAACP could claim a membership of some 400,000, larger by far than at any previous time, with more than a thousand branches spread all over the country. The Association had become for the first time a truly nationwide organization, large-scale in character, not only speaking for but actually representing Negroes from all strata of the community. It was, even as the Communists were to concede, the foremost movement for Negro rights developed in the United States. From its new prestige and alliances the

NAACP had gained self-confidence. For the first time it could view the future without having to worry about survival.

The Communists, on the other hand, although recapturing some of the popularity they had enjoyed during the United Front period, could point to few gains—and many losses— among Negroes. The NNC, SNYC, ILD, and NLVC did little about the upsurge of Negro discontent except try to sit on it. They failed to turn it to account as they might have done had they not soft-pedaled the colored man's grievances "to win the war." A basically revolutionary movement that could take no-strike oaths, support labor conscription, applaud the con- viction of non-Communist leftists as seditionists, and offer the right hand of fellowship to the National Association of Manu- facturers—all to save its fatherland from defeat by the Nazis —would certainly be able, in the same cause, to reduce its militancy about the rights of America's fifteen million Negroes. But having done so, the comrades should not have been sur- prised to find Negroes regarding them with something less than unrestrained fervor.

V

The Immediate

Postwar Period

WITH the publication of the Duclos letter in April, 1945, the Kremlin signaled another switch for the Communist Party in the United States. Comrade Duclos charged that dissolution of the party in May, 1944, and the establishment of the Communist Political Association were serious mistakes, constituting a repudiation of Marxist philosophy and the tenets of Leninism-Stalinism. Publishing the Duclos letter in full in the *Daily Worker*, the National Board of the CPA shortly afterward convened in emergency session and adopted a resolution calling for a comprehensive review of Communist activities since June, 1941, on the basis of the "friendly criticism" of the French comrade. Admitting Duclos's charges, the CPA confessed that it had been guilty of "opportunism," "revisionism," and "social-democratic" tendencies. The governing body then called for a debate on the whole program of the past four years; the debate would be conducted in club meetings and in the pages of the *Daily Worker* and other Communist publications, primarily *Political Affairs*. A more apt phrase than "debate" would have been "collective confessional." Finding a demon was essential; Earl Browder was slated to play that role.[1]

[1] Earl Browder, "Stalin Ruined the American Communist Party," *Harper's*, CCXX (March, 1960).

Keenly aware of their neglect of the Negro and of their failure during the war period to stand up for racial rights, the participants had some explaining to do. Most of them sought to justify their action, or rather inaction, on the grounds that an aggressive program would have interfered with the war effort. Ford, for example, admitted that he had created illusions among Negroes that if they refrained from protest in wartime, they could expect to receive "democratic rights gratis from Roosevelt and the Democratic Party." Ford, it might be pointed out, had served as vice-president of the Negro Labor Victory Committee and was prominent in the councils of the CPA. Another Negro comrade, Edna Lewis, who was active in the East Harlem Branch of the CPA, criticized the National Board for succumbing to "Browderism" and vacating its "special responsibility to the Negro people." George Lohr, not to be outdone, confessed that the Communists had committed many tactical errors "which hampered the struggle for the rights of the Negro people." And so the spectacle unfolded, with members and leaders alike flinging themselves on the mourners' bench to pour out their sins.

In late June, 1945, the CPA called an emergency national convention. At its conclusion the Communist Party of the United States was reconstituted. The resurrected party adopted resolutions in which it emphasized the collective guilt of Communists in failing to press for Negro rights in employment, the armed services, civilian defense, even the Red Cross Blood Bank. Summing things up was the following declaration: "The opportunist errors of our former general policy limited the effectiveness of Communist work on the Negro question." Especially damaging, it was now admitted, had been the "glossing over" of the "national character of the Negro question" and the unwarranted illusion "that the big bourgeoisie themselves would carry forward after V-E Day the wartime gains of the Negro people." [2]

[2] Ford, "Revisionist Policies," p. 7.

The Communists flagellated themselves because they had "soft-pedaled" the fight against the "inferior status" of Negroes in the armed forces; in fact, they pointed out "that even before the Duclos article we had been forced to reevaluate and adjust our position." Just what the adjustment had been was not specified; certainly no definite, concrete actions were cited. Few confessors could point to protests registered by them during the war interval. There had been, the party admitted, a loss of confidence in the party among Negroes, a sharp decline in Negro membership, and a failure to secure replacements for disillusioned black comrades. Such observations conveyed the impression that the CP had at one time recruited a substantial colored membership and enjoyed wide respect among non-Communist Negroes; such was not the case. Many Negroes might have been aware of Communist activity regarding the race question, but only a few—never as many as seven thousand at any one time—had joined the party. Among those who did affiliate there was a high turnover. After the war it was patent that even the meager achievements of the past were no longer possible.

The party confessional was superfluous as far as the NAACP was concerned. The Association's national officers had pointed out the error of Stalinist ways frequently during the preceding six years. Although the patency of the party's wartime choice was such that it could not seriously hope to recapture its Negro following of the United Front period, here and there—in those trade-unions which the party controlled, in a few NAACP branches it had captured, and in such moribund agencies as the ILD, NNC, and SNYC—it retained bases from which it sought to renew its bid for Negro support.[3] As a matter of course, Communist attacks on the NAACP were renewed in spite of the fact that the Association did during the war what the comrades now confessed they should have done.

[3] *Amer. Negro in CP*, pp. 4–6.

The NAACP leaders were disturbed about the Communist campaign in the immediate postwar period, not because they believed the party had or could secure a significant Negro following, but because the label of "Communist" might be pinned on the Association by its conservative opponents. The label might frighten away potential Negro members and discredit the NAACP in the eyes of the larger community. The rapid development of the cold war and the near-hysterical reaction of considerable segments of the American public to the alleged internal "Red" menace made it relatively easy for various groups, from whatever motives, to characterize most forms of Negro protest as Kremlin-inspired. Three centuries of Negro loyalty and patriotism and the NAACP's forty years of legitimate, responsible efforts to obtain Negro rights could not always counter such charges effectively. Other equally responsible organizations had similar experiences.[4]

The party recognized that the possibility of penetrating the top echelons of the NAACP was remote. Realizing that issues could be befogged at the local level and knowing that the Association's national officers, because of their basic commitment to democratic procedures, would crack down on local branches only as a last resort, the Communists hoped to penetrate branches and thus accomplish through the NAACP what they could never achieve under their own banner. A part of the CP strategy was to attack the executive secretary and the national NAACP Board all along the line.

During this period the CP's designs on the NAACP took several forms. Although the organization as such was not subjected to the intense vituperation of the 1941–1945 interim, the leaders were continuously criticized, in accordance with the tactic of "progressive protest from below," by which the party hoped to change the NAACP's program to its own advantage at the local level and to lay the groundwork for unseat-

[4] J. C. Record, "Red-tagging of Negro Protest," pp. 325–333.

ing or hobbling the national officers and staff. The Communists recognized, as did the NAACP leaders themselves, that many of the local branches were weak and unstable, since much of the wartime protest fervor had been diluted. Moreover, the inexperience of local leadership operated in the CP's favor. Thus there was an opportunity for party functionaries to move in and bid surreptitiously for branch leadership and eventual control.[5]

Attacking from another direction, the Communists proposed joint actions between their own local units and the NAACP branches. This would have provided the former with the stamp of respectability and an opportunity to rail against national leaders of the Association when they frowned upon or actually attempted to prohibit such collaboration.[6] Even though the party was increasingly hard put to find allies, as sentiment against it crystallized in the trade-unions, political organizations, and racial and nationality groups and as the federal government acted to weaken it through both legislative and administrative measures, it remained highly critical of the NAACP national officers and staff members. Only when its failing strength forced the issue did the party's approach change.

Returning veterans were another group to which the party hoped to appeal. Believing that former Negro soldiers were largely unaware of the party's wartime role, knowing that veterans' organizations such as the American Legion and the Veterans of Foreign Wars frequently practiced Jim Crow, and convinced that colored veterans were discontented with their lot in postwar American, the Communists initiated the United Negro and Allied Veterans of America (UNAVA). Although the organization received some support from non-Communist

[5] Alfred Baker Lewis, "The Problem of Communist Infiltration," *Crisis*, LXI (Dec., 1954).

[6] NAACP, *Labor Manual*, p. 70.

groups, was endorsed by a number of religious and fraternal organizations, and included non-Communist Negro veterans, the party's control was established early and never relinquished.[7] However, the UNAVA was largely sterile during its several years of life. A different result might have developed had its Communist orientation not become increasingly clear, leading to the withdrawal of most of its non-Communist supporters who had regarded it initially as a legitimate agency for guarding Negro veterans' interests.

The UNAVA's chances were limited also by the sensitivity of the NAACP to the needs of returning Negro soldiers. Establishing a Veterans Affairs Office in the national headquarters, the Association developed a special program not only for handling their claims but also for drawing them into activities of the local branches. Veterans' committees were set up in the branches, and it was largely to those rather than to the UNAVA that Negro ex-servicemen turned for assistance.

The UNAVA was organized in April, 1946, with Kenneth Kennedy, a former SNYC functionary, as national commander and George Murphy, Jr., who was to become a publicist for the Progressive Party in 1948, as acting adjutant. The new organization reportedly got off to a fast start. In March, 1947, it claimed a membership, almost entirely Negro, of five thousand in twenty-two states. In May the national commander reported that within the preceding two months its numbers had grown to ten thousand in thirty-one states. Murphy, who became identified with a whole series of front organizations during the postwar period, succeeded Kennedy as national commander.[8] The party directed some of its most able young men

[7] For example, Joe Louis was named honorary national commander, and Jackie Robinson agreed to serve as a member of the National Advisory Board of UNAVA. Judge William C. Hueston was listed as honorary national judge advocate.

[8] House Committee on Un-American Activities, *Appendix to Hearings*, 84th Cong., 2d sess., Part II.

into the UNAVA and tried to use it as a recruiting instrument for the CP and other organizations. The UNAVA, however, was unable to maintain its initial momentum, partly because Negro ex-soldiers showed little disposition to join any of the veterans' organizations. By the time it made the Attorney General's list of subversive organizations in 1949 the UNAVA was well on the way to oblivion; it did not survive the official classification very long. The failure of the Communists to make headway among Negro veterans was a salient setback.

A major party handicap was its revival of the self-determination doctrine, which was once again offered as the fundamental approach to the Negro question in the United States. Although there had always been considerable reluctance among colored Communists to adopt this Kremlin-fathered offspring, and such knowledgeable spokesmen as Doxey Wilkerson and Francis Franklin had firmly opposed it, the concept was reinstituted at the behest of the northern-born urban whites who controlled the CPUSA. Paradoxical it was that they who knew so little about Negroes and even less about the South took it upon themselves to offer the "conclusive" definition of the "Negro nation" in the Black Belt.[9]

NAACP officials must have observed with amazement the reappearance of that old chestnut. Shaky from the start, the self-determination doctrine was being undermined further by industrialization of the southern region and large-scale migration of Negroes to the North, East, and West. As in the past, the success of the party among Negroes, such as it was, occurred in spite of this fundamental guide to the Communists' racial program. As the party was increasingly forced to take the defensive, it found the doctrine an albatross, which it could not throw overboard because it might incur the wrath of the Kremlin skippers. Moreover, since the party's reem-

[9] Doxey A. Wilkerson, "The Negro and the American Nation," *Political Affairs*, XXV (July, 1946), 652–658.

bracement of the self-determination theory was part of a general reaction against the "revisionism" of the war period, the American comrades had an emotional investment in the switch-back to Negro nationalism.

An interesting development during this period was the party's concern about anti-Negro feeling among white party members. Official cognizance of the problem was first taken in central directives, later in party magazines and newspapers. Local unit leaders were urged to discuss "white chauvinism" regularly at meetings and to "educate" or, if necessary, to take disciplinary action against members deemed guilty of racial discrimination in either private or public actions.

It is difficult to determine how extensive intraparty racial prejudice and discrimination actually was. Most of the evidence is provided by the Communists themselves; it consists primarily of examples from local units here and there and charges by a few disaffected Negro former members. No systematic survey to gauge the nature or amount of anti-Negro behavior within the ranks was ever announced by the party.

In the *Daily Worker* and *Political Affairs* there were extensive discussions, and these sources give the impression that racial prejudice was, indeed, widespread. It now appears, however, that the "virus of white chauvinism" was not nearly so virulent as these official organs suggested. The importance party leaders and journalists attached to the issue was, in all probability, part of a reaction to their wartime neglect of the Negro question and must be seen in the wider context of confession and rededication.

By overdrawing instances of internal prejudice against Negroes, Communist spokesmen hoped to reaffirm the party's commitment to racial equality. In doing so, they could underscore their atonement for prior errors and at the same time perhaps create a more favorable image of the party among prospective Negro members. But even such aims do not fully explain why so much was made of the issue or why the discussion sometimes bordered so closely on the ridiculous.

Among party members discrimination reportedly took several forms: white members signed restrictive covenant agreements, arbitrarily removed Negro comrades from local elective posts, refused to meet with or speak to Negroes in some clubs, threatened to expose Negro members who refused to renew affiliation, segregated education classes on the basis of color, and punished Negro breaches of party discipline severely even though whites were rarely called to account for the same violations.[10] Thus in its own internal structure, the self-proclaimed "party of racial equality" apparently had a long way to go. Such practices were suspected or known to at least some Negroes outside the organization and reinforced their skepticism.

The NAACP had pointed out previously that the party's claim to internal racial equality left something to be desired. For example, it had noted that Communists on occasion had used white women in an effort to lure Negro men into their units. "In a very real sense," one NAACP official remarked in an interview, "the Communists operated on exactly the same assumptions as prejudiced southern whites who were convinced that the foremost desire of Negro men was sex relations with a white woman." [11] Nolan has made some rather penetrating observations along the same line, indicating the conflicts which such techniques engendered among the Negro and white women in the party's local units.[12]

Internal racial prejudice had always been a problem for the CP; bringing it into the open during the postwar period was an indication not so much of its novelty as of a heightened con-

[10] Pettis Perry, "Destroy the Virus of White Chauvinism," *Political Affairs*, XXV (June, 1946), 1-5.
[11] Interview, anonymous, Chicago, Aug., 1955.
[12] *Op. cit.*, pp. 121-122.

cern about it. Perhaps party leaders sensed that with the loss of strength in the unions, they needed Negro support more than ever. By publicizing internal prejudice, and at the same time underscoring action taken to eliminate it, the Communists set out to prove they were firmly committed to internal equality.

By that time the NAACP rarely had to deal with the problem of anti-Negroism among its white members. Since the Association's single goal was to remove racial barriers, it espoused no over-all political ideology; therefore whites would join only if they were dedicated antidiscriminationists to begin with. This is not to say that there were no interracial tensions within the NAACP. But the very purpose of whites in joining in the first place was to give concrete expression to equalitarian sentiments. Although they might object to some of the Association's tactics or withhold full support in certain instances, the basic requirement for affiliation was a rejection of color prejudice, coupled with a general commitment to try to eliminate it within the framework of the Association's program and methods. Unlike the CP, the NAACP had no reason to hang onto white members who did not share such sentiments.

Through the years the Association learned that in the long run Negro gains must come primarily through their own efforts, though there might be whites in power who had good intentions toward the race.[13] As the NAACP recognized the limits of interracial cooperation and conciliation and moved more in the direction of broad economic and political action, it had less need for those whites, however well-intentioned, who might mediate between NAACP members and the Caucasian power elite. As a firmer base from which to bargain becomes established and the principle of equality receives legal sanction, the NAACP's need for sympathetic but hard-headed white members may increase. They will be of a type somewhat

[13] Lawrence, *op. cit.*, p. 79.

different from those on whom the Association has depended in the past.

The structure of the NAACP was a weapon against the party's bid for Negro support. The Association was an essentially centralized organization with major authority residing in the Board of Directors. Until the revision of the NAACP constitution in 1945, the Board theoretically and actually was all-powerful and self-perpetuating. While it allowed a large degree of autonomy to the branches on specific local issues, it could make its impact felt by withholding funds or by refusing to give active support to endeavors that it disapproved. In some cases, of course, the Board because of strong grass-roots sentiment was forced to go along with actions that it would have preferred to stop or to postpone. (For example, it is questionable whether or not the NAACP's Board of Directors would have initiated the school segregation cases or pushed them as vigorously as it did in the absence of strong demands by the southern branches.)

In the past the annual conventions had not been gatherings where delegates representing all shades of opinion fought about and reached decisions on basic policy questions. Those delegates who did attend were frequently selected on the basis of their capacity to finance at least a part of their expenses to and from the "conferences" (not at that time "conventions"). The less affluent members of local organizations, whose expenses in many cases could not be borne by the branches, had less opportunity to express their views directly. Further, the conferences, as Lawrence has pointed out, were primarily occasions for inspirational speeches, spiritual communion, and publicizing the work of the NAACP among wider audiences, Negro and white.[14]

The modifications of the NAACP constitution in 1945 changed somewhat but did not really diminish the powers vested in the

[14] *Ibid.*, pp. 89-90.

Executive Board. Theoretically, the annual convention became the highest legislative body, and its decisions presumably were binding on the Board and the staff until the following year. But the proceedings were subject to review by the Board of Directors, and if two-thirds of its members did not approve any item, it could send a memorandum to local branches setting forth the disagreement; whereupon the branches would conduct a referendum on the issue. However, there was no certainty that the Board would consult the branches in this fashion, since it enjoyed a wide discretion in interpreting resolutions and policy statements of the convention and in selecting those on which it would act.

The Board also retained the power to amend the constitution under which it functioned.[15] It thus had the technical means to change election and convention procedures to perpetuate itself indefinitely and to get rid of dissenting elements. But even if ethical considerations had not restrained Board members, there was the hard fact that, unlike a trade-union with a closed-shop contract or a military organization with compulsory obedience, the NAACP is a voluntary association which will be supported by Negroes only when considerable individual and branch autonomy is allowed. In the matter of local autonomy, however, the Board was careful to distinguish between racial and organizational issues, and when the latter were at stake, it moved against the threatening elements, especially the Communists.[16] In the circumstances the latter had no recourse except to set up rival organizations. This they attempted in the immediate postwar period even while trying to penetrate the Association from below.[17]

[15] NAACP, *Constitution of the NAACP* (New York: NAACP, 1957), art. XII, p. 12.

[16] Lewis, *op. cit.*, p. 586; West Coast Regional Office, NAACP, *Organization and Conference Manual* (1957), Appendix.

[17] *Communist Campanile* (Berkeley, Calif.), VI (May, 1949), 1.

The dominant position of the NAACP Executive Board was also apparent in the process of selecting convention delegates. They were chosen by local branches, but were likely to be those persons who were favorable to the national leadership and in agreement with existing general policies. This circumstance minimized the chances of representatives following an independent course and the possibility that opposition factions would form either prior to or during the convention. Selection of delegates could be influenced by favorable publicity in *Crisis*, pressures from regional and national staff members, and other means—in short, by those devices that large-scale, voluntary organizations characteristically employ to develop and maintain essentially one-party internal government.

The NAACP's own "county unit system" is an interesting development. It enhanced the power of small branches at the expense of large ones. No branch, regardless of size, had more than ten convention votes, and the smallest had a minimum of two. Thus a branch with 20,000 members (Detroit) had no more electoral influence that did five small branches whose total numbers might not exceed 250. By getting the support of delegates from the smaller branches, which were likely to be more impressed by and dependent upon the national office anyway, the incumbent officers and staff could push through policies that might have been rejected by the majority in an equal representation system.[18]

Why would the Board sanction for the NAACP the very kind of voting system for which the NAACP so roundly denounced the state of Georgia? The Board's reasons were not wholly self-serving. Taken into account were smaller units' fears of being snowed under by the big city branches, which

[18] An interpretation of Article II, Section 3 (c), and of Article IX, Section 2 (a), by the Board of Directors of the NAACP modified somewhat the extreme disproportions, but the essentials of the county unit system within the organization remained.

might adopt policies unacceptable to them. NAACP leaders also were concerned lest large branches fall into the hands either of self-seeking politicians [19] or of radical political groups, especially Communists. Another consideration was the wide geographic distribution of NAACP branches. Those in the South frequently had only weak ties and haphazard communication with the national office and with other local units in and outside the region. It was believed that they must be given an important voice in the Association to strengthen their loyalty and involvement. In any event, the structure has been one of the hurdles facing the CP in its efforts to penetrate the NAACP. Indeed, some NAACP officials have expressed the conviction that they could have waged a much more hard-hitting campaign against the Stalinists had they been willing to use fully the powers vested in the Executive Board and the national staff.[20]

The chance that Communists could get control of the Executive Board by persuading its members to accept a Stalinist philosophy and program was always remote. Here and there the CP got an individual member to endorse a specific action or participate in what turned out to be a front organization. Had the CP captured enough large branches, it theoretically could have pressed its will upon the Board by curtailing Board funds and other means, but the actual branch structure and branch-Board relations are not so neatly maneuverable.

Moreover, Communist branch leaders would have had to

[19] A good example of such political troubles is the 1960 election in the San Francisco Branch of the NAACP, in which strong political factions and leaders contested for control of the organization. Suspension of the election by the National NAACP Board of Directors was necessary pending an investigation and resolution of the impasse (*Bay Area Independent*, Jan. 7, 1960, p. 1; *Sun Reporter*, Jan. 23, 1960, p. 1).

[20] Interview with Gloster Current, director of branches, NAACP New York, Aug., 1955.

deliver on some immediate issues to retain their leadership; and they would have had to obscure their ultimate intent. Either would have been difficult to accomplish. The NAACP's national office was increasingly disposed to move in, revoke charters, and reorganize local branches when Communists were even momentarily successful. In 1950 the Association adopted a policy of prohibiting membership to Communists; it also strengthened the hand of the Executive Board and national staff in dealing administratively with threatened branches.

In spite of such barriers the Communists made renewed efforts to get inside the NAACP. Their most notable success was their persuasion of Du Bois (who, after more than a decade at Atlanta University, returned to the national staff) to support their "peace" and "progressive" slogans enunciated at the outset of the cold war. They also kept the control of some local branches which had been achieved during the war years. Renewing their efforts among students, they were successful in infiltrating some of the college branches. Their limited success in the colleges must be seen as a result in part of the NAACP's ineffectual youth and student program. That program was unchallenging to most young Negroes, who, in addition, disliked the restraint exercised by the adult branches and lacked any strong voice in policy determination. Members of the national staff and the Executive Board were attacked by the CP through some of the college chapters. On the whole, however, this criticism was uncoordinated. It was not shared by many of the adult branches and hence had little change of being effective.

One reason for the party's concentration on race in general and on the NAACP in particular was its loss of strength among other organizations. Within trade-unions affiliated with the CIO there was a growing determination to eliminate Stalinists from leadership positions and, if necessary, even from membership. Although the party had built a number of front organizations among racial, nationality, ethnic, intellectual, and cultural groups, its real strength had been in the left-wing unions of the CIO. With both internal and external pressures being exerted against them there, the Communists looked about for other allies; they hoped to find them among the Negroes, whose militancy carried over from the war period. At the same time, of course, the party was under increasing attack from state and federal agencies, its status as a legal organization continuously being questioned.

The National Negro Congress, meeting in Detroit in May, 1946, spoke rather kindly of the NAACP, although noting the presence of leaders who were not progressive or "close to the Negro masses." The party concluded that the 1946 meeting represented a real "rebirth," although it had never indicated publicly before that the organization was not alive and active.[21] It was the NNC's (and the party's) intent to establish a string of local councils across the nation along somewhat the same pattern as in the United Front period. Although the NNC demanded fair employment practice legislation (which traced back to the hated MOWM and Randolph), abolition of the poll tax, and antilynching legislation, it naturally opposed any attempt to check the spread of communism in Eastern Europe, Africa, the Middle East, and Asia. It insisted that the realization of Negro rights in the United States was inseparable from the forward march of the "People's Democracies" and that American Negroes had a responsibility to support these countries, thereby opposing American foreign policy.[22]

No significant growth followed the "rebirth" of the National Negro Congress. Its Communist composition was well known, as the NAACP again pointed out when the NNC faithful gathered in Detroit. The Association warned its own mem-

[21] John Pittman, "The Negro People Spark the Fight for Peace," *Political Affairs*, XXV (Aug., 1946), 726.

[22] *Ibid., passim.*

bers to have nothing to do with the NNC. As the congress tried to counterpose American Negroes to Truman's foreign policies, its self-righteous overtures to the Association were rejected flatly.

In fact, the NNC could function only in those communities where the party had a strong union base. Within less than two years after its rebirth the NNC was so ineffectual that it was merged with the ILD and other organizations to form the Civil Rights Congress (CRC).[23] Thus the NNC was not so large a threat to the NAACP as it had been during the United Front period. Outside of a few urban areas the Association could safely ignore its activities and concentrate on its own program.

The Southern Negro Youth Congress lasted a little longer than did its parent organization, holding on until after the fiasco of the Progressive Party in 1948. In a number of southern communities such as Birmingham and Richmond it remained active and staged two southern conferences in the immediate postwar period. Although weakened during the war, it maintained a number of its councils in urban centers and in Negro colleges and universities. Its continuing Communist orientation was indicated by the resolutions adopted at the conferences and the directives issued from its Birmingham headquarters, denouncing the Truman doctrine, the Marshall Plan, and so on.[24]

That the SNYC did concern itself with regional problems is indicated by its intervention in some of the more dramatic violations of Negro rights in Tennessee, Georgia, and Alabama. Following the Columbia, Tennessee, race "riot" in 1946, it conducted an investigation and sought to raise funds for the defense of the Negro victims. Its failure to account for the

[23] Dorothy K. Funn, testimony, House Committee on Un-American Activities, *Investigation of Communist Activities in the New York City Area*, May 4, 1953, quoted in *Amer. Negro in CP*, p. 11
[24] W. Record, *op. cit.*, pp. 249–251.

amount and use of the money, however, led to its being criticized by the Southern Regional Council and the NAACP. Both intervened in the trials and successfully defended Negroes charged with law violations which were, in fact, the products of local white citizens and law enforcement officials.[25]

More and more the SNYC was thrown back on other Communist-oriented organizations such as the United Negro and Allied Veterans, the Mine, Mill, and Smelter Workers, and the Southern Conference for Human Welfare. By this time the SCHW was pretty much under Stalinist control, although it continued to receive the endorsements of some non-Communist labor and liberal spokesmen who still hoped the organization could be salvaged. Lacking the ability to follow through on specific problems, the SNYC produced few concrete results after stirring up a publicity controversy. On several occasions it dropped significant cases, leaving the NAACP to pick up the pieces and do what it could.[26]

Its overtures to the Association were either ignored or flatly spurned. Individual Association members participated in SNYC councils, offering advice and even serving as sponsors or endorsers of Youth Congress conferences. However, they acted in individual capacities and largely because of sentimental attachments to the young men and women in the SNYC caught up in the throes of postwar racial protest. No doubt some of the sympathizers from the NAACP were dissatisfied with the Association's student and youth program in the South and hoped that young Negroes might find some organized expression of their concern for racial justice in the SNYC. It should be emphasized, however, that the NAACP members who participated were few.

[25] NAACP, *Terror in Tennessee* (New York: NAACP, 1946); SRC, *What Happened at Columbia* (Atlanta: SRC, 1946).

[26] Interview, anonymous, Birmingham, Ala., Sept., 1955; interview anonymous, Atlanta, Ga., Sept., 1955.

In early 1948 the SNYC endorsed the Progressive Party and used its limited resources (supplied largely by the CP-oriented unions) in behalf of Wallace and Taylor. With the failure of the Progressive Party to make a significant showing in the South and among Negroes generally, the SNYC's fate was sealed. In December, 1948, it was dissolved, and its remaining members were advised to join regular or student branches of the NAACP. The Association, however, was not particularly eager to accept them, especially those who might enter the college or youth branches. NAACP field secretaries were told to advise branch officials to screen and keep an eye on the young transfers. Following the dissolution of the SNYC, its executive secretary, who was not a southerner, incidentally, joined the staff of the Progressive Party in New York and later became editor of *Freedom*, a monthly publication designed to carry the Communist message to Negro workers.[27]

Experiencing a similar fate was the Southern Conference for Human Welfare. Having lost most of its non-Communist trade-union support, largely boycotted by southern churchmen, educators, journalists, and students, and under heavy fire from investigating committees and conservative southern papers, the SCHW by 1948 was on its last legs. It tried to hang on by establishing a series of state committees to deal with local situations more effectively, and its Southern Education Fund was able to survive.

The passing of the SCHW marked the end of the initial high hopes of southern liberals, Negro and white, which the late Charles S. Johnson had expressed so eloquently a decade before.[28] Of course, the noble dream had really died long before, and the demise of the SCHW brought merely a belated funeral. The SCHW's all-out support of the Progressive Party had further alienated those Negroes who realized that a third-party

[27] This publication is no longer being issued.
[28] "More Southerners Discover the South."

movement, which spoke eloquently of racial justice but had little to offer in the immediate, practical alleviation of the Negro's economic plight, could but lead them up a blind alley.

In an effort to liquidate its old organizations in the civil rights field and to form a new one free of the Communist stigma, the party in April, 1946, merged the old ILD with the Federation for Constitutional Liberties to form the Civil Rights Congress. For a time it appeared that the new agency might become an effective rival of the NAACP since it proposed to give considerable attention to issues affecting Negroes. However, the CRC was established for other purposes as well, primarily to defend Communists and their sympathizers before investigating committees, administrative agencies, and courts. It was used also as a means of embarrassing the American government in the eyes of colonial peoples.[29]

The bulk of CRC financial and political support came from the CP and the left-wing unions it controlled. There was some backing from the NNC, UNAVA, and SNYC, but these organizations were so weak in funds that they could offer little more than moral and ideological support. There was an attempt to develop extensive working relationships between the NNC and the CRC, but the former, in spite of its boasts, was becoming increasingly a paper organization. In December, 1947, the NNC was quietly merged with the CRC, writing finis to an organization that a decade earlier had drawn the loyalties of a number of non-Communist Negroes who visualized a concerted nationwide racial movement as a means for dealing with the fundamental questions troubling colored men.

One index of the CRC's party orientation was the naming of William L. Patterson, the executive secretary of the old ILD, to a similar post in the new organization. Underscoring the nexus further was the fact that such men as George Addes, then the top left-wing leader of the UAW; Hugh Bryson, presi-

[29] CRC, *We Charge Genocide* (New York: CRC, 1951).

dent of the Marine Cooks and Stewards Union; Lee Pressman, the former general counsel of the CIO, who later was to reveal his long-time party membership; and Paul Robeson were named vice-presidents. Initially, however, a number of liberals, Negro and white, with a principled concern for civil liberties endorsed the CRC and were active in some of its local units. As its Communist character became increasingly apparent, they tended to drop away. NAACP officials feared the CRC; they surmised that it would reinstitute the tactics followed by the ILD in the Scottsboro and similar cases. They assumed that the CRC would become the major party instrument in the civil rights area and that it would receive greater Communist backing than had the other organizations with which they had dealt in the post-war period.

In a manner reminiscent of the ILD, the CRC intervened in a number of trials in which gross injustices to Negroes were clearly evident. The cases of the Ingram family (Georgia), the "Trenton Six" (New Jersey), and Willie McGee (Mississippi) provided dramatic examples of the violation of Negro rights in court procedures. In the Ingram case the NAACP handled the defense and raised funds for that specific purpose. While having no direct hand in the case, the CRC conducted money-raising drives, rallies, and, through the Communist parties of other countries, protest demonstrations. It seems reasonably certain that most of the money raised by the CRC in the name of the Ingrams was used for them, though some of it was probably diverted to the defense of Communists then on trial in Judge Medina's Foley Square court.[30]

In the Trenton Six cases the CRC intervened and secured a reversal of the lower court's decision on grounds that the indictments had been obtained illegally. However, the *Daily Worker*, as it had in the Scottsboro case, claimed that "mass pressure" from workers and "the Negro people" was what

[30] Nolan, *op. cit.*, pp. 85–86.

really turned the trick. The CRC proceeded to take some relatives of the accused on a nationwide speaking tour, staging meetings and demonstrations in which funds were raised for fighting the cases further. How much of the money was actually used to defend the six accused Negroes is not known, but it is not unreasonable to assume that at least a part of it went for unrelated propaganda work and for the defense of Communists under indictment in federal courts.[31]

The Trenton defendants were eventually freed; some of their cases were handled by the American Civil Liberties Union and the NAACP.[32] The CRC again claimed that their acquittal was a result of "mass pressure" and contrasted the effectiveness of the CRC in the Trenton Six trials with the failure of the NAACP in the Ingram case. Ignored was the fact that the former was held in New Jersey and the latter in Georgia; furthermore, there was no mention that the CRC's side-line activities in the Ingram case had been a distinct handicap to the Association's effort. Essentially the same procedures were followed in the McGee case, with sums of money being raised but not fully accounted for.

By 1950 the CRC was badly in need of friends and would have accepted even moderate civil rights organizations, whose methods it had ridiculed and against which it had competed in its zest for cases having propaganda promise. Circumstances now forced it to make overtures in their direction. The NAACP officialdom had felt the sting of CRC invective even while the latter was declaring its willingness to work with "progressive" elements in the Association. At the local level the CRC had sought to embarrass and pressure NAACP branch leaders by offering "unity" proposals and then branding the officers as "uncooperative" and "misleaders" when they refused them.

[31] *Ibid.*, pp. 86–87.

[32] Daniel Webster Wynn, *The NAACP versus Negro Revolutionary Protest* (New York: Exposition Press, 1955), p. 51.

These were old devices that party organizations working among Negroes had employed off and on over the years. Even at its height, however, the CRC attack never approached that of the ILD in the early days of Scottsboro. Its overtures were nonetheless rejected, and the Association moved to the offensive.

The conflict between the CRC and the NAACP came to a head in late 1949 and early 1950. With a number of other nation-wide organizations, the NAACP planned a National Civil Rights Mobilization to be held in Washington, D.C., in February, 1950, to coordinate the efforts of racial, ethnic, labor, religious, and political groups on the civil rights legislative front. The impressive character of the move, in which the NAACP played a central role, mirrored the growing ability of the Association to form effective alliances and to broaden its concerns to encompass issues not exclusively relating to Negroes.

Prior to the Mobilization meeting William L. Patterson, the CRC's executive secretary, requested that his organization be invited to participate fully. Roy Wilkins, then acting secretary of the NAACP and chief planner of the conference, turned Patterson down. Moreover, Wilkins used the occasion to reiterate NAACP opposition to the whole Communist ideology and apparatus, including the CRC. Fashioning a little history lesson, he pointed out to Patterson that the CRC was only the ILD in new dress and that the Association's leaders had been vilified by both.

He reminded Patterson of Communist attempts to undermine the NAACP in the name of "unity," which the Association had never wanted and would not have now. Then, switching to the Communists' wartime behavior, Wilkins castigated them for being all too willing to sacrifice the immediate welfare not only of Negroes but of others as well. The NAACP leader no doubt was letting off a long-building head of steam. There was method in his public wrath, however, for the Association needed to forestall irresponsible charges that the Mobilization was Communist-inspired. Moreover, he was preventing in advance the almost certain split which would have come at the first session had the Communists been invited or admitted. He was determined that the Stalinists should not put the death sign on yet another coalition of liberal forces.[33]

Unable to participate in the Mobilization openly, the CRC attempted to infiltrate the gathering by sending party activists as delegates from other organizations, even from NAACP branches where possible. This required an issuance of credentials by the few party-controlled branches to members and even nonmembers. Fake credentials from paper organizations were also used in the hope that Stalinists would be certified before the ruse was discovered. Suspecting that such tactics might be employed, the Mobilization planners established a sophisticated credentials committee; Willard Townsend, A. Philip Randolph, and Herbert Hill, the astute NAACP labor secretary, all of whom were conversant with CP tactics and personnel, spotted and barred all but a few of the Communists, regardless of the guise in which they appeared.[34] Those who did get through were quickly isolated, and in some cases their credentials were revoked. This demonstration of the NAACP's attitude toward Communists and the CRC was unmistakable.

The Communists reacted in characteristic fashion, charging that NAACP leaders had succumbed to the "offensive of Wall Street," "wavering" and "petty," they were bent on the "subordination of the Negro people's liberation movement to the

[33] Roy Wilkins, letter to William L. Patterson, executive secretary CRC quoted in *New Leader*, XXXII (Dec. 24, 1949), 1.

[34] Interviews with Willard Townsend, Chicago, July, 1955; with Herbert Hill, San Francisco, Oct., 1957; with A. Philip Randolph, New York City, Aug., 1955; and with Gloster Current, New York City, Aug., 1955.

overall strategic and tactical aims of American imperialism."
Having failed to force its way into the Civil Rights Mobilization, the CRC became even more alone. Moreover, it could
build no effective following of its own. Had the NAACP cooperated with it, or even remained neutral, the CRC might have
lasted longer. Instead, the Association took the offensive and
at the national and branch levels battled the CRC openly, effectively challenging the Stalinists' efforts in the whole civil rights
arena.

Stimulating NAACP opposition to the Communists were attempts by the latter to capitalize Negro discontent in behalf
of the Progressive Party (PP) in 1948 and afterward. The PP
was initiated largely by Communists and controlled by them
through most of its brief career. In line with the CP's methods,
the PP placed great emphasis on the Negro question and made
the issue focal in its campaign. It publicized racial injustices
and promised to do something about them; it secured endorsements from a few outstanding Negroes representing a wide
range of political opinion; it nominated Negro candidates for
state and federal offices and for local posts in those cities where
Negroes were a significant political element; it attracted a few
Negro politicians—but it had little appeal for Negro voters.
The PP's general showing, and especially its failure to dilute
Negro loyalties to the Democratic Party, apparently shocked
the Stalinists in November. Following its traditional course,
the NAACP refused to endorse any party but tried to persuade
the Democratic and Republican organizations to adopt platforms that, if carried out, would benefit Negroes. Indicative
of the NAACP's attitude toward the PP was its dismissal of Du
Bois when he attempted to use *Crisis* and the Association itself
as a means of strengthening what Henry Wallace described
as Gideon's Army.[35] Defining their problems primarily as eco-

[35] *Crisis*, Oct., 1948; interview with Roy Wilkins, acting executive
secretary, NAACP, Berkeley, Calif., Dec., 1948.

nomic and conceiving the Democratic Party as the best choice in the circumstances, Negro voters turned their backs on both the GOP and the Progressives.

The NAACP interpreted the Progressive Party's appeals to Negroes as chiefly attempts to put the race in opposition to Truman's anti-Soviet foreign policies.[36] The CP was apparently interested primarily in a defeat of the Democrats, on the theory that the isolationist elements in the Republican Party would force it to pursue a much less vigorous program of foreign economic and military aid when it came to power. As the campaign progressed, there was less hope that the PP could win a large number of votes in any quarter, although some observers thought it might make inroads on the Democratic Party's Negro following in the North. With that the Communists would have been gratified had it led to Republican victories in the pivotal states.

NAACP leaders were concerned about that possibility, fearing that it might lead to the defeat of northern liberals, isolate Negro voters, vitiate their bargaining power, and lend the old charge of Communist influence some substance in the public view. As it turned out, of course, the fears proved groundless, the PP obtaining fewer than 1,200,000 votes and Negroes everywhere going overwhelmingly Democratic as they had in 1936, 1940, and 1944. Although the NAACP was by no means ecstatic over the Truman "miracle," it was encouraged by the belief that Negroes had made the best choice in the circumstances and had refused to be taken in by Progressive maneuvers.

The CP had attempted to push the NAACP toward the Progressive Party through Du Bois, who had returned to the Association in 1944. He was active in behalf of the PP—so outspoken, in fact, that the Executive Board moved to dismiss him in September, 1948. Other considerations were involved.

[36] *Crisis*, LV (Dec., 1948), 361.

Although both the NAACP and Du Bois had changed, Du Bois never fitted in again as he had in the early days. Had Du Bois continued, NAACP members of a conservative political persuasion would have been affronted, and the Stalinists might have had an opportunity to infiltrate the top echelons of the organization.

In 1949 the Communists tried to secure the adoption by the Association convention at Los Angeles of a series of resolutions. The CP had captured the Long Island (Jamaica), New York, branch, and through its delegation proposed: (1) censure of the Executive Board's endorsement of the Marshall Plan, (2) disapproval of aid to non-Communist countries through the ECA (although the resolution was couched in different terminology), (3) nonsupport of the new Atlantic Pact, (4) reinstatement of Du Bois in his former position or appointment to a similar one, (5) establishment of a review committee to scrutinize failure of the NAACP to use its full resources to secure Negro rights, and (6) authorization of local branches to form alliances with other organizations if the Executive Board failed to bring about greater efficiency and branch participation.[37] Knowing that such proposals were going to be offered, the Executive Board through *Crisis* and the national staff cautioned branches to select delegates representative of Negro rather than left-wing political interests and attacked the CP outright.[38]

If adopted, the measures would have crippled the NAACP. First, the Association would have been committed to the CP's foreign policy line. Second, the door of the national office would have been opened for Communists and their sympathizers to move into responsible staff positions. Third, the Executive Board would have been discredited and national staff members placed in jeopardy, for a review board in which

[37] *Crisis*, (June, 1949), 185–186.
[38] Editorial, "The NAACP and the Communists," *Crisis* (March, 1949)

Stalinists participated would scarcely have found much to laud in either group. Fourth, the extension of more autonomy to local branches in the form proposed was aimed at giving the Stalinists a chance to pick them off one by one. Subsequently they could have operated as party fronts, with lessened fear that the national office would crack down, revoke charters, or reorganize the branches under non-Communist officers.

Concerning several of the proposals the Communists were in a somewhat favorable position. On foreign policy measures they were at a disadvantage since their intent was rather clear and should have been readily detectable by even the most naïve delegate. But on the question of reinstating Du Bois the Communists had a better stance because of his long prestige; he was well known and his past services well recognized. With respect to the establishment of a review committee and the granting of more autonomy to local branches, Communists expected considerable support from those who, from a variety of perspectives, thought that too much power was vested in the Executive Board and national staff.

In control of the Resolutions Committee, however, were anti-Communists representing varying shades of organizational interests and political orientation. Only two of the resolutions—those on the ECA and the Atlantic Pact—ever reached the floor, and they were beaten by substantial majorities. A vote for the measures was not necessarily indicative of Communist sympathy; to some of the delegates the questions were of little significance, and for others foreign aid programs per se seemed unattractive in the face of so much poverty among Negroes at home.

Wilkins, who was presiding, then offered to put the other proposals to a vote of the convention, but he warned their advocates that he and others would take the floor and expose their backers fully. Communists had little stomach for that, being already convinced of an overwhelming defeat. Although

Wilkins could have used the occasion for belaboring the Communists, he chose to deal with them by other means, wanting to avoid, if possible, the unfavorable publicity that would follow any public cognizance of the presence of even a few Communists in NAACP ranks. Public confrontation he was prepared to employ only if the party spokesmen did not subside.[39]

Of course, the Executive Board would scarcely have countenanced the resolutions had they somehow been adopted. They would have been ignored or submitted to referendum after a vigorous campaign to obtain their defeat. As an ultimate tactic the Board might even have amended the constitution, which it had the power to do, in such a way that the resolutions would not have been binding. It is not likely that such drastic measures would have led to the defection of many non-Communist members or local branches.

It was in 1949, also, that the NAACP took sharp public notice of the party's penetration of some local branches by infiltration and by the manipulation of unsophisticated leaders. The aim of the Communists, declared an editorial in *Crisis*, was not to build a better NAACP but to operate one more front group to confuse and embarrass Americans and the American government in the world contest of ideologies. The editorial then described the tactics likely to be used by the Stalinists and suggested how they could be countered. Few criticisms of the Communist Party in this country, from whatever source, have equaled the NAACP's denunciation. Moreover, the source in this case was important since it was an organization which was committed to democratic values and racial rights and one which had fought the Communists at all times and even for its very survival.[40]

Prompting the condemnation was a series of developments

[39] Interview with Roy Wilkins, Berkeley, Calif., Jan., 1949.
[40] "The NAACP and the Communists."

culminating in the party's capture or infiltration of some branches in the East, the Midwest, and the Far West. Two conditions usually obtained where this occurred: (1) the branches were located in cities where the party had a fairly strong trade-union base, and (2) the branches were relatively new or had grown quite rapidly during the war and postwar periods. While the NAACP leaders were disturbed over Communist activities in some of the college chapters, their main misgivings concerned the large urban branches where the lack of experienced leaders and the presence of many southern migrants attracted the shrewd tactics of Communist followers.

The West Coast experience gave substance to such fears. As early as 1947 the Regional NAACP Conference adopted a resolution calling on affiliates to scrutinize carefully all candidates for branch offices to make sure that non-Communists were elected or appointed. Here was a difficult task because party followers, Negro and white, tried to conceal their identity on entering the Association's branches. It was sometimes impossible for local members to differentiate clearly between those whose interest was genuine and others whose participation was party-directed. Although the resolution together with similar statements probably stirred up unwarranted suspicion of fellow Negroes, it also alerted local officers and members to organizational problems posed by the Stalinists.[41] It led the local NAACP leaders to cooperate more closely with other non-Communist civil rights organizations in exchanging "intelligence" on individuals suspected of having party ties.[42]

[41] NAACP, West Coast Regional Conference, 1947, *Report of the Resolutions Committee*, San Francisco, March 7–8, 1947 (San Francisco: NAACP, 1947).

[42] Interviews with NAACP officials in San Francisco, Denver, Chicago, Detroit, Cleveland, and New York City, summer, 1955.

The national NAACP's fears were reinforced by the party itself when it openly urged members to overcome the "sectarian tendencies" which led them to attack the NAACP openly and to avoid participation in it in previous periods. Such avoidance, the party warned, strengthened the Association's reformist and social-democratic leadership and nullified potential Communist internal influence. Misunderstanding the "central role played by the Association in Negro life," doctrinaire comrades, the party proclaimed, were all too prone to ignore its possibilities. Calling for a careful reexamination of the NAACP, the party directed its members to intensify their efforts to steer the former onto a truly "progressive" course. Unable to destroy the Association, to establish effective rival organizations, or to penetrate it from the top, the Communists were left with the alternative of boring from within and from below.[43]

Until 1950 NAACP leaders were satisfied that Communist infiltration could be dealt with adequately through the measures previously described. However, public sentiment both Negro and white was becoming increasingly sensitive to any charges of influence. Although the party had made no large-scale inroads in NAACP branches, the presence of any Communists and their control of even a few of the hundreds of local units were continuing sources of embarrassment. The NAACP, given time and using its slower, informal methods, could have contained and eventually eliminated the Communists, but its leaders felt sharper techniques had become essential.

At the 1950 convention held in Boston the NAACP adopted, by a vote of 309 to 57, a resolution empowering the national

[43] Edward E. Strong, "40 Years of the NAACP," *Political Affairs,* XXIX (Feb., 1950), 23 and *passim,* and "The Till Case and the Negro Liberation Movement," *ibid.,* XXXIV (Dec., 1955); Rosser, *loc. cit.*

office to expel any unit which, "in the judgment of the Board of Directors," should or had come under Communist or other political control.[44] The opposing vote, one-seventh of the total, as Nolan has pointed out, gave the impression that Communists were that large a minority in the organization. Nolan went on to suggest that not every delegate who voted against the anti-Communist resolution was a party member or even a sympathizer; moreover, the fact that the convention was held in Boston enabled the party to muster its eastern seaboard followers as delegates in numbers far out of proportion to their membership.[45] The adoption of a resolution with "teeth" in it was a defeat of the first magnitude for the Communists, who responded in characteristic fashion. But they were already on the wane and could do little more than noisily deplore what took place.

Although the national office of the NAACP has not made extensive use of its expulsion powers under the new policy, the 1950 resolution again warned local leaders about Communist machinations and gave the branches specific recourse if they felt threatened. Already the powers of the Executive Board were so broad that, had it chosen to do so, it could at any time have revoked the charter of any Communist-captured branch. However, it had been reluctant to use its authority because for private organizations such as the Association, dependent for funds primarily upon its members and committed to democratic values generally, expulsion is a distasteful measure. Not only is there the stamp of dictatorship in high-handed charter lifting; the national office needs local dues. Branches have folded and died too frequently; keeping existing ones vigorous is no easy matter; reorganizing a branch is a costly, time-consuming process. Depriving Negroes even momentarily

[44] NAACP, *Annual Report*, 1950 (New York: NAACP, 1950).
[45] Nolan, *op. cit.*, pp. 179–180.

of an agency through which they might protest effectively is a matter to be weighed carefully by those who have the power.

Always there has been the belief, with a few exceptions, that whatever the difficulty within a branch, even CP infiltration, it could be handled through less dramatic means. Significantly, the NAACP did not have to resort to the self-amputation finally used by the CIO in ridding itself of Stalinists. Viewed in the over-all context, the actions of the 1950 NAACP convention must be adjudged a public gesture to protect the organization's good name, a warning to the Stalinists to keep hands off, and an educational device for its own members.

More important than the resolution itself were subsequent actions taken by the national office, regional directors, and officers of larger branches. The Association specified the organizations with which its local units could not cooperate; included were the party and its various front organizations. Special instructions listing the left-wing agencies that branches would be likely to encounter in a particular activity or area of interest were prepared for local officers and committee chairmen.[46]

Although it was not widely publicized, regional and local officials developed, in cooperation with other civil rights organizations, other moderate Negro organizations, and anti-Communist trade-unions, informal intelligence systems through which dossiers were compiled on party activists and information on Communist maneuvers was exchanged. In that way the Stalinists and their sympathizers were more readily spotted, their moves were anticipated, and a coordinated opposition was worked out. It was through such a procedure that the Michigan civil rights and fair employment practice drives staged by non-Communist organizations, including the NAACP, were freed of party interference and influence. The

[46] NAACP, *Labor Manual*, p. 70.

effectiveness of such lesser measures explains in part why the Association did not have to employ the ultimate power authorized by the 1950 resolution and reaffirmed at subsequent conventions.

Encouraging the NAACP's overt anti-Communist moves in 1949 and 1950 was the fact that within the CIO relations between party followers and their opponents finally reached the breaking point. In the early postwar years the CIO had censured the Communists and adopted resolutions expressing disapproval of their tactics. However, Philip Murray, fearful that their expulsion would disable the organization, urged unions under CP leadership to "clean their own houses." That did not occur, at least not on a scale sufficient to avoid a showdown. In some unions—for example, the United Automobile Workers, the United Steel Workers of America, and the United Packinghouse Workers—where there were strong party factions, the Communists were defeated. In others, such as the National Maritime Union and Transport Workers Union, where the Communists were in control, their hold was broken by the apostasy of the left-wing chiefs themselves. During the power struggles Communists made special appeals to colored workers, frequently charging that the opposition was racist and predicting that if "progressive" leaders were curbed or eliminated, racial discrimination would spread. Such charges were difficult to substantiate since the anti-Communist factions usually had as good, and in many cases better, equalitarian records than did the Stalinists. Particularly damaging to the latter was their wartime underplaying of racial grievances.[47]

Although the NAACP was not formally involved in the intraunion conflicts, it generally supported anti-Communist factions, and in certain crucial situations its influence on Negro workers had a significant bearing on the outcome. On the

[47] Kampelman, *op. cit.*, pp. 35, 41, 214.

other hand, the Communists were not above building anti-Negro factions where prejudiced white support might enable them to retain their grip. In a few situations where Communists controlled a local NAACP branch, they attempted to use it to strengthen the "progressive" elements in the strife-torn trade-unions. The NAACP's influence in those struggles was heightened by the presence on the Executive Board of a number of strong anti-Communist labor leaders.

In a dozen or so unions the party's grip could not be loosened, and the CIO eventually expelled them. In some instances—the Tobacco, Agricultural and Allied Workers, the Mine, Mill and Smelter Workers, the International Longshoremen's and Warehousemen's Union, the Marine Cooks and Stewards Union, and the United Electrical Workers—there were substantial Negro memberships which, if aligned solidly for or against the left-wing leaders, might have carried the day.

In the MMSW, the leftists were so firmly entrenched that the CIO could not break their hold on the membership by establishing a competing organization. The MMSW had a relatively good record on Negro rights. To the advantage of the Stalinists also was the further solidification of the membership by the peculiar social structure and culture of mining communities. Similar considerations help explain the continued vigor of the Longshoremen after the expulsion.[48] The UEW presented a somewhat different picture, and it is noteworthy that when the CIO established a rival organization in the electrical industry many Negroes went over to it.

In some instances the alternate available to Negroes who might have chosen anti-Communist leaders had little to recommend it. A Negro's anticommunism would have had to run exceedingly deep to make him select Harry Lundeberg's Sea-

[48] Jane Cassels Record, "The Rise and Fall of a Maritime Union," *Industrial and Labor Relations Review*, X (Oct., 1956), 81–92.

farers' International Union, with its historic racialism, over the left-wing Marine Cooks on the West Coast, which had an excellent record for intraunion racial equality.[49] In such instances the position of the NAACP was ambivalent. It could neither deny that the party-lining union had "delivered" for Negro and other minority group members nor suggest palatable alternatives in the immediate situation.

It is significant that the NAACP branch in San Francisco filed an *amicus curiae* brief with the National Labor Relations Board protesting the racial policies of Lundeberg's SIU when it was trying to capture the left-wing MCSW membership in the early 1950's. Only under pressure from the Association's national office, which feared the Communist label, did the local NAACP chapter withdrew its brief. The SIU was able to win the representation election only because the NLRB changed the bargaining unit. Overwhelmingly the votes of the Negroes and other minorities went to the left-wing union, the NAACP's reticence notwithstanding.

The Communist problem did not shake the NAACP nearly so much as it did the CIO. Proportionately there were many fewer Stalinists in the former; moreover, they held no positions of any consequence at the national level, and they controlled relatively few of the branches. Unlike the CIO, the NAACP was not compelled to expel any large units, and it was not necessary to suspend or reorganize many of them. There was little possibility that the adoption of a vigorous anti-Communist program would lead to substantial losses of members or funds. Had the risk existed, the NAACP's leaders might well have shown the same hesitancy as did Philip Murray in moving against them. But getting rid of Communists was an almost unqualified boon to the NAACP's growth; where it failed to expand numerically, the reasons were unrelated to its handling of the Communists.

[49] *Ibid.*

Although the hard-line Stalinists could take their unions out of the CIO or, more appropriately, retain a partial hold on some of them when they were expelled, the party had no such alternative in the NAACP. There simply were no solid groups of followers to join such an exodus. The Communists protested the NAACP's internal anti-Stalinist moves, but they could do little toward establishing an independent Negro movement. So they were forced to continue their efforts to penetrate the NAACP, the only tactic with even the remotest possibility of success in maintaining some voice in racial movements. And the Association's countermoves had made that possibility remote indeed.

Thus even before the outbreak of the Korean conflict the party's influence among Negroes generally and in the NAACP specifically had hit a new low. In several local branches, however, the Communists still had some nuisance influence. Although they could not exercise any determinant voice in the Association's policies, they were still capable of evoking, or at least giving some small substance to, an unfavorable public image.

As in other instances, the Communists appeared willing to endanger, even vitiate, an organization they could not control. In pursuing that course they had few reservations about the means employed and few concerns about the fate of those organizations and their members whose control was their objective.

VI

Since 1950

THE experience of the Communist Party in the United States since 1950 has been one of decline to the point of almost total disintegration. The precise nature and course of that decline cannot be comprehended without sustained reference to the organization's work among Negroes. Particularly instructive is the party's relation to the National Association for the Advancement of Colored People, which has continued as a virile force on the race relations scene. Essential, too, is an appreciation of the internal dynamics of the NAACP and of the external forces that played upon it and influenced its responses to the party.

During the past dozen years there have been no abrupt shifts in the Communist Party's position on the Negro question; one finds no examples of those sharp turns of policy and program that occurred in 1928, 1935, 1939, 1941, and 1945. Even if such quick changes had taken place, their consequences would have been minimal because of the temper of the times, a dwindling of party membership, and a consequent inability to follow through with effective action. In the NAACP no profound changes have been made in the direction of new programs or in the internal distribution of power and influence.

The interaction of the NAACP and the CPUSA during the

1950's and early 1960's has taken place in a context of crisis and change that caused the party to wage a struggle for survival and the NAACP to become an even more powerful and stable force in American Negro life and in American race relations. The party has continued its ambivalent attitude toward the NAACP, sometimes eagerly seeking support, at other times bitterly attacking the Association and its leaders. The NAACP increasingly has regarded the party not as a challenger but as an irritant and a source of embarrassment. Particularly has this been the case since 1955.

By the early 1950's the general course of both organizations and their relations with each other were fairly well set. Their lines of development could have been drastically altered only by the most profound social and political upheaval. Even the death of Stalin and the Khrushchev succession, the differences that rather quickly emerged between the Russian and Chinese Communists, and the many other developments in world communism did not affect significantly the career of the CPUSA, which had become so weak that even had the USSR demanded a bright new course of flight, there could have been only token flapping of the clipped wings. The NAACP, on the other hand, because of its background, structure, composition, and basic orientation was in a position to pursue even more vigorously the programs of previous years. New tactics were developed, but basic goals and strategies bore remarkable similarity to those of the past. New challenges, such as were presented by black nationalist movements, particularly by the Black Muslims, appeared. A number of direct-action, nonviolent movements expressed through organizations such as the Southern Christian Leadership Conference and the Congress of Racial Equality made an impact on both the Negro and white communities—and on the NAACP. But the NAACP's response was rather typical of an established protest organization. It modified some of its techniques. It did not—indeed, it

170

could not—alter substantially its basic character and structure; nor did it need to do so.

Since 1950 American Communists, whose ranks were continuously thinning, have sought to capitalize racial unrest and racial militancy in two distinct but closely related ways. First, they attempted to enlist Negro support, as they had in the past, for foreign policies of the USSR and to direct their resources against those aspects of American foreign policy deemed harmful to the Communist-bloc nations. Second, they tried to rebuild their strength in those areas where they were suffering the greatest and most important losses: the trade-unions and race organizations. In both efforts, but especially in the latter, the Communists came into sharp conflict again with the NAACP, which adopted increasingly stringent methods to prevent Communist infiltration of its own ranks and to combat Communist-controlled organizations among Negroes.

Of course, the party was under attack from many other quarters—courts, legislative committees, trade-unions, and the major political parties—each contributing to the decline of the party in some particular area. Its encounters with the NAACP and the resulting defeats must be seen in this context; otherwise one is likely to overestimate the resourcefulness of the Association. Because of the liberal-humanist bent of most of its leaders, the NAACP was not comfortable with many of its fellow crusaders against the party. For example, extreme patriotic organizations, such as the Daughters of the American Revolution, had little in common with the Association and did not share its definition of crucial issues or concur in its goals. Members of legislative committees that investigated Communists rarely endorsed the NAACP program or pushed measures that it advocated. But it was in method that the greatest disparity existed between the NAACP and such anti-Communist gladiators as the House Un-American Activities Committee. Most Association leaders are essentially civil libertarians, who believe that the struggle against communism—like the struggle against white supremacy—should be pursued within the framework of the Bill of Rights.

Important to an understanding of more recent CP-Association relations is a review of some developments in the late 1940's and early 1950's which helped shape the course of what followed. Among the more significant events was the indictment of the top leaders of the Communist Party under the Smith Act. In that episode one finds a clear example of how the Communists sought to exploit broad issues of race relations as a means of perfecting organizational defense and of carrying out their commitments as spokesmen for world Communist interests. One sees also the patterns of involvement with the NAACP and the way in which the conflict was carried on.

One of the Communists' first responses to the indictment was a greater effort to secure backing from Negroes, and they went about it in such a way that conflict with the NAACP was inevitable. However, the party hierarchy could scarcely have anticipated the countermoves the NAACP would take or the vigor with which they were pursued. Since some of the Communist defendants were colored, one of the main strategies was to try to link defense of individual Communists in the courts with defense of Negro rights.[1] The trial of the "Top Twelve" and the subsequent appeal of their convictions consumed many months, during which time the Communists made extensive

[1] National Committee, CPUSA, "The Court of Last Appeal Is the American People," *Political Affairs*, XXX (Oct., 1951), 1–3; Eugene Dennis, *In Defense of Your Freedom: Summation in the Trial of the Eleven Communist Leaders* (New York: New Century Publishers, 1951), Introd. by Elizabeth Gurley Flynn, *passim;* George W. Crockett, Jr., *Freedom Is Everybody's Job: Summation in the Trial of 11 Communist Leaders* (New York: National Non-partisan Committee to Defend the Rights of 12 Communist Leaders, n.d.); House Committee on Un-American Activities, *Report on the March of Labor* (Washington: 1954), *passim*

use of their standard legal and propaganda devices and developed some new ones for the occasion.

Their main technique was to emphasize that what was at stake in the trials was not the right of a revolutionary organization to violate basic rules of the political community, but the right of all Negroes in America through organizations of their own choosing to realize those opportunities and responsibilities essential to full citizenship. That was a new approach. The defendants were portrayed as symbols of and spokesmen for the legitimate aspirations of the race. The *Daily Worker* and other party publications linked instances of racial discrimination to the alleged injustices perpetrated in the trials against the party and its leaders. An attempt was made to refurbish and expand the old tactic of "mass pressure" on the courts and "mass protest" as a legal weapon. The public mood of the late 1940's had changed from that of the 1930's, however, and the responses of non-Communist civil libertarians were disappointing to the defendants at New York's Foley Square courtroom and in other courts.

Another novel tactic was to fill the courtroom with Negro spectators. In addition to their own followers the comrades tried to gather other colored folk en masse. Negroes were called on to stage demonstrations, have their organizations adopt resolutions, write individual letters of protest, and in other ways condemn indictment and conviction of the Communist officials. According to the party, Negro rights and Communist rights were inseparably linked; denial of the latter was equivalent to repudiation of the former. This theme ran throughout Eugene Dennis' summary and plea at Foley Square, and it characterized party activity during the appeals to higher courts.[2]

As a part of its strategy the party retained Negro lawyers as members of the defense battery. It called Negro defense

[2] Dennis, *op. cit., passim.*

witnesses, who were allowed wide latitude in their testimony
and who emphasized the party's concern for racial justice.
Among the witnesses at Foley Square was Doxey Wilkerson,
a Negro educator and one of the most sophisticated second-
echelon spokesmen, who was later to break with the party.
In an effort to create a favorable public atmosphere for the trial
of the top leaders, the party had its members attend court
sessions and stage local demonstrations.[3] It charged that the
real crime of the three Negro defendants—Davis, Jackson,
and Winston—was in having been born black and then daring
to fight for racial freedom. Special emphasis was put on the
fact that Davis had been a member of the New York City
Council, elected from a district composed largely of Negroes.
The Communists did not, however, mention that Davis' election was possible only because, under a system of proportional
representation, white voters from outside Harlem actually determined the choice; the Communists had mustered their followers from all over the city to ensure his victory, making this
their primary objective. They were extremely disappointed by
the fact that the jury, drawn by lot, included three Negroes.
That fact removed any chance that effective propaganda could
be made of an all-white jury, which might have struck a responsive chord among Negroes.

The prolonged and frequently tedious maneuvers elicited
little support from Negroes. The NAACP, although it had been
urged to intervene in behalf of Jackson, Davis, and Winston
on the basis of race rights, refused any part in the trial. Somewhat ironical was the fact that the Communists now called
upon the Association to employ in their behalf those principles
and skills they had so vociferously condemned over the years.
While many NAACP leaders and members believed that the
Smith Act was an unconstitutional infringement of political
freedom, they did not discern in the law or in the trial itself

[3] Nolan, *op. cit.*, pp. 189–190

any racial prejudice. As civil libertarians they had misgivings; as racial spokesmen and protest leaders, who time and again had been subjected by the defendants to the most extreme denunciation, they viewed the proceedings with somewhat mixed feelings. Certainly the ultimate test of the Association's commitment to civil liberties might have been passed had it taken up the cause of the "Top Twelve" at Foley Square.

Although the party failed to win any significant support from leading non-Communist Negro leaders at the trial, it was able during that era to fasten its hold more firmly on Paul Robeson and W. E. B. Du Bois and to exploit their popularity in its "peace" and race concerns. At Peekskill, New York, Robeson had sought to give a concert which was to be also a rally for the Foley Square defendants. Party members were taken to Peekskill in an effort to offset the protests of the local "patriotic" groups. Rioting ensued. In Paris, Robeson was moved to declare before a "peace" rally that fifteen million American Negroes would not fight against the Soviet Union in the event of war between Jim-Crow America and the "stronghold of racial equality." The implication to at least a segment of the American public was that Negroes were pro-Soviet and pro-Communist, which was probably the effect the party had hoped to achieve.

Although Robeson was repudiated by practically every American Negro spokesman of national stature, including Walter White of the NAACP, Lester Granger of the National Urban League, and Jackie Robinson, the Negro major leaguer, the damage was difficult to repair; the harm and embarrassment to the moderate organizations themselves, although indirect, was nonetheless real.[4] In somewhat the same way, although with less fanfare, Du Bois made statements and participated in front organizations in a way that seemed to indicate to his

[4] *Ibid.*, p. 194, see also House Committee on Un-American Activities, *Hearing*, July, 1949, 81st Cong., 1st sess., p. 481.

former associates that his searching intelligence and critical faculties had declined. Robeson and Du Bois were, however, only individual propagandists; they were not key leaders either in the party or in the organizations through which it attempted to reach Negroes.[5]

The Communists continued the work of the Civil Rights Congress, whose repudiation by the NAACP has already been described. They also attempted, with little success, to build new organizations among Negroes. In June, 1950, along with a number of front organizations and some party-controlled unions, the Stalinists sponsored the National Trade Union Conference on Negro Rights (NTUCNR). Although some local NAACP members participated in the gathering, none of the branches gave official endorsement. Knowing the sponsorship, the national office of the Association would not authorize any form of official involvement. Prior to the meeting of the NTUCNR the party had established a number of Negro labor councils on a local basis, and it was through them that some of the delegates were recruited. There had been no nationwide apparatus bringing the labor councils together in a central organization.

Establishing a continuing committee, the NTUCNR tried to lay the groundwork for concerted activity among Negro workers, and the committee was directed to explore prospects of a permanent organization. Composed of either Communists or Communist sympathizers among minor Negro labor leaders, the committee proceeded to establish additional Negro labor councils, claiming that between June, 1950, and October, 1951, twenty-three such units had been started in "major in-

[5] Robeson was chairman of the editorial board of *Freedom*, which spoke for the National Negro Labor Council, a party-controlled instrument operating among Negro trade-unionists. However, the publication was run by the late James Burnham, once executive secretary of the Southern Negro Youth Congress.

dustrial centers throughout the country." The committee issued a call for an organizing convention, which was held in Cincinnati in late October. About 1,500 delegates, "from the mines, from the mills, from the shops, from offices and classrooms, Negro working class leaders, and rank-and-file members, organized and unorganized," were said to have given enthusiastic backing to the formation of a permanent National Negro Labor Council (NNLC); they then returned to their homes, a party journalist wrote, determined to man their "battleposts and girded for action to attain economic, political and social status equal to white people," and to "make America a better place for all people." [6]

Prior to the Cincinnati meeting the NAACP, the NUL, and spokesmen for non-Communist trade-unions called attention to the Communist origins and composition of this latest front organization among Negro workers. Some NAACP members journeyed to Cincinnati, but they did so without authorization of either the national office or its local branches. However, in listing their affiliations and in publicizing their organizational activities, party spokesmen tried to convey the impression that these delegates had official sanction at least at the local level.[7] The list of sponsors and delegates carried a number of NAACP identifications, but the party protected itself by inserting in extremely small print at the bottom of the list a note that the organization tags were for purposes of identification only. It is possible that in a few instances, where members and officers were unaware of the party's influence in forming the NNLC, delegates did have some form of NAACP branch acquiescence.

Through the *Daily Worker* and other party publications,

[6] *Freedom*, I (Nov., 1951), 1; see also Anita Bell Schneider, testimony, House Committee on Un-American Activities, *Investigation of Communist Activities in the San Diego, Calif., Area*, July 5, 6, 1955, 84th Cong., pp. 2606–2630.

[7] "These Were the People on the Freedom Train," *Freedom*, I (Nov., 1951), 4.

notably *Freedom*, a monthly tabloid-type newspaper published by "Freedom Associates," the Communists, beginning in 1950, sought to convey the impression that many NAACP branch leaders were dissatisfied with the Association and its national staff and were seeking a more militant instrument for pursuing racial rights.[8] The organizing convention of the NNLC provided a good example of this tactic, which was to be used again.

Among the NNLC resolutions at Cincinnati were demands that the federal government drop its indictment of Du Bois, restore in full Paul Robeson's passport rights, intervene to free members of the Ingram family illegally imprisoned in Georgia, repeal the Smith and McCarran Acts, end discrimination in the armed forces and government agencies, and liquidate American colonialism.[9] Such goals, on the surface, might have been approved by a great many non-Communist civil libertarians. However, here they were linked with more controversial demands and supported forcefully by spokesmen of the "independent" party-controlled unions recently expelled from the CIO. The NNLC, for example, was very much opposed to United Nations intervention in the Korean conflict, and it wanted a truce and withdrawal of the American forces. Moreover, it wanted to stop American economic and military aid to the non-Communist countries of Europe and Asia, including Chiang Kai-shek's Chinese Nationalists.[10]

The NNLC was able to expand its activities for a time after the founding convention, primarily where the left-wing unions were relatively strong. It could do little elsewhere, especially in the South, where even the moderate labor organizations were having a difficult time organizing the unorganized workers, white or black. Its intention of organizing sharecroppers and agricultural workers in the cotton belt and elsewhere was unrealized. In Chicago, New York, Cleveland, Detroit, Cincinnati, and San Francisco the strongest local councils were estab-

[8] *Ibid.*   [9] *Ibid.*   [10] *Ibid.*

lished. However, the NNLC could elicit little support outside the expelled CIO unions and other groups the party controlled or strongly influenced.

One reason was the existence in many cities of relatively strong NAACP branches. The latter not only refused the now rather palsied left hand of fellowship, but also exposed, sometimes quietly and at other times loudly, the party origins of the council.[11] On occasion, the NNLC was able to stir up something of a ruckus, particularly in the political field. For example, it sent its spokesmen before local and state legislative bodies, where in the course of their testimony they emphasized their left-wing connections, knowing full well that this would probably militate against ameliorative measures.

Generally, however, non-Communist, pro-civil rights organizations such as the American Civil Liberties Union and the Association of Catholic Trade Unionists were able to isolate the NNLC leaders and divorce themselves publicly from them. Where civil rights measures were adopted, it tended to be in spite of their advocacy by the NNLC. In a few instances, notably in Chicago, the NNLC was able to convey the image of cooperation between itself and some of the other organizations in the field of race rights. But when it was placed on the Attorney General's list of subversive organizations, its Communist character received wider notice, especially in the Negro and labor press.

Horace Cayton, sociologist and long-time student of racial movements, dissected the NNLC tellingly in his columns in the *Pittsburgh Courier;* George Schuyler, an old critic of the party among Negroes, spelled out the composition of the council; and the late Willard Townsend, who, in addition to

11 For example, the NAACP publicly repudiated the National Negro Labor Council in hearings before the Board of Supervisors of San Francisco, which in 1951 was considering a fair employment practice ordinance.

being president of the "Red Caps" union, a vice-president of the CIO, and high in the councils of the NAACP, was also a newspaper columnist, gave the NNLC a periodic working over in his weekly syndicated column. Herbert Hill, knowledgeable labor secretary of the NAACP, who had helped bar the Civil Rights Congress representatives from the National Civil Rights Mobilization in 1950, carried the fight against the council to Negro labor groups and NAACP branches over the country. Perhaps more than anyone else he was responsible for the failure of the council to make headway among Negroes in local trade-unions.[12]

The Association's leaders did not fear that many of their own members would be won over by the NNLC. They were disturbed, rather, by its possible appeal to unlettered Negroes and by the nuisance role it might play in the NAACP's efforts to build cooperative relationships with non-Negro organizations. Having had some rather sad experiences along those lines in Michigan and California, where its efforts to secure fair employment practice legislation had been obstructed by Communist intervention, the NAACP went to great pains to isolate the NNLC and to divorce itself publicly from it.[13]

Reacting to the NAACP's drive against the NNLC, the Communists tried to devise an effective counteroffensive. By that time a direct organizational attack was thought inexpedient. Instead, a fresh effort was made to discredit Association leaders. For example, an article in *Freedom* in March, 1952, was headlined: "Memo to NAACP Leaders: It's Time to Fight—Not Fawn." Its author, writing under the name of Claude Blanchette, referred to the exclusion of Communists from statewide civil rights mobilizations, which the Association helped

[12] Pettis Perry, "Certain Prime Aspects of the Negro Question," *Political Affairs*, XXX (Oct., 1951), 11.

[13] Interview with executive-secretary, Detroit Branch, NAACP, Aug., 1955.

organize in half a dozen states, and claimed that NAACP officials had "held their fire against the post-war big-shots, severely
limited the participation of Negroes in the program, and excluded representatives of all organizations not originally among
the signers." Walter White, the NAACP's executive secretary,
was singled out for special criticism. Blanchette concluded that

> if we are to have civil rights then the rank and file members of
> the NAACP and all its co-operating organizations are going to
> have to make their leaders start *fighting* for freedom and stop
> *fawning* over smug pro-war politicians and comfortable labor
> leaders.[14]

In an editorial, "Cadillac Leadership," *Freedom* attacked
Dr. Channing Tobias, veteran member of the NAACP Executive Board and a United States delegate to the United Nations;
the editorial questioned the right of Negroes like Tobias and
Edith Sampson, a Chicago attorney, to speak for Negroes in
opposition to the Soviet Union. "This should be a warning,"
it continued,

> to leaders of our established organizations, Messrs. White and
> Wilkins of the NAACP, Mr. Granger of the Urban League: you
> may follow the Sampson-Tobias line if you will, cry "Red"
> every time Negroes mass their strength to fight against lynching,
> poverty, and war. That way, you may land a job in the diplo-
> matic corps and achieve the highest goal within the grasp of
> our Cadillac leadership. But by the same token you will lose
> the right and ability to play a part in the magnificent struggles
> which are at hand and which will lead to our freedom, as surely
> as the day follows night.[15]

These Communist attacks on the NAACP through *Freedom*
and the National Negro Labor Council were elaborated in

[14] Claude Blanchette, "Memo to NAACP Leaders," *Freedom*, II
(March, 1952), 1.
[15] Editorial, *ibid.*, II (March, 1952), 1.

the *Daily Worker, Political Affairs,* and other party outlets.[16] Running through all the charges was a general theme: the Association's leaders had betrayed the struggle for Negro rights, traded racial interests for personal recognition and power, toned down the expression of Negro unrest, dampened the genuine radicalism of the colored masses, and betrayed the Negroes to the Democratic Party, the prowar and anti-Soviet politicians, and the business unionists. To offset this, the Communists preached, militant Negroes and rank-and-file members of the NAACP must realize that if the organization was to serve the case of racial justice, they would have to push the existing leadership toward "genuine" action or else get rid of it. At that time the CP's Negro membership was less than 1,000; the Association's was more than 300,000.

Even while it was calling upon NAACP members to follow the true path to enlightenment, the party was questioning whether it itself might not have strayed off course. Writing in early 1952, John W. Preston lamented in *Political Affairs* that

serious right opportunist and "left" sectarian errors are creeping into our work especially as it relates to the mass organizations such as the N.A.A.C.P., Elks, and churches. The decline in the N.A.A.C.P. work during the period under review (1950–1952) has been noted. This we must take steps to correct in the period ahead.[17]

Under the sub-heading of "Struggle against Negro Reformists" Preston noted that the activities of the NAACP leaders were declining because of their "policy of servile support to the foreign and domestic policies of Wall Street." Lester Granger, Roy Wilkins, Willard Townsend, A. Philip Randolph, Benjamin Mays, and Channing Tobias—with the exception of

[16] Samuel T. Henderson, "White Chauvinism and Negro Bourgeois Nationalism" (II), *Political Affairs,* XXXII (Jan., 1953), 62–63.

[17] "Recent Developments in the Negro Peoples Movement," *Political Affairs,* XXXI (Feb., 1952), 42.

Granger, all high-ranking Association leaders—were accused of "unparalleled" demagoguery in their "capitulation to the [cold] war policies of the bourgeoisie." Walter White was excoriated for "diverting the Negro masses" to support the Truman administration and "American imperialism." [18]

In few instances when the Communists attacked the NAACP and its leaders, particularly after the outbreak of the Korean War, was there a failure to charge them with being anti-Soviet, prowar, and imperialist. The Communists continued to insist that no racial issue, regardless of its limited and unique character, could be divorced from American foreign policy; and the latter was condemned as long as it did not complement the interests of the USSR. This underscored again the American CP's subservience to the Soviet Union and demonstrated the incidental character of its concern with racial matters. If the NAACP had tried to gather American Negroes behind Russian foreign policy, its leaders would almost certainly have been transmuted overnight into great racial statesmen, even if they suddenly fired Thurgood Marshall and his whole legal staff— and embraced Mississippi's governor Ross Barnett as a long-lost brother!

The Korean wartime "line" on the NAACP echoed an estimate of the organization offered by Edward E. Strong in February, 1950, a few months before the war erupted. Strong conceded that a number of important changes had taken place in the Association in recent years: an increase in working-class elements, a spread of local branches over the South, a diversification of membership, and the building of a record of "many positive achievements." It is interesting that a party official could acknowledge such gains while castigating the leaders primarily responsible for them. In trying to do both, Strong explained that the successes were real but now the Association was in crisis, due to the "failure of the national leadership to

[18] *Ibid.*

conduct mass struggles, involving the whole membership, around the burning issues confronting the Negro people." [19] The failure of the reformist leaders was being countered, Strong reassured his readers, by the "emergence of a powerful Left, anti-imperialist, anti-fascist current among the Negro people which is clearly discernible in the NAACP." [20]

If that was the case, Strong supplied no evidence, and it must be conjectured that he was voicing a hope rather than stating a fact. At the very time Strong's article appeared, the NAACP had already taken steps to eliminate the few Stalinists from its ranks and to prevent their reentry in different garb. The 1950 convention had given the national office authority to expel any branch which the national board found upon investigation to be "under Communist or other political control and action." The party could count its Negro membership only in the hundreds, and its race organizations were growing steadily weaker.

Of course, there was a strong anti-Fascist group in the NAACP; indeed, it comprised practically all the members. The dominant sentiment was "anti-imperialist," too, if the word means opposition to the exploitation of colored colonial peoples. But one searched in vain for the NAACP's "powerful Left" factions, by which Strong meant, of course, Communists and their followers. If a few had managed to hang on or slip back in, they were conspicuously quiet. Here and there they might sound off and stir up an occasional controversy in a local branch, but the strength of the Stalinists had been tested when they tried to capture the Los Angeles convention in 1949 and to retain their influence in the Boston convention in 1950; their efforts had not amounted to much. Whistling-in-the-dark claims, such as Strong set forth, could not conjure up leftist

[19] "On the 40th Anniversary of the N.A.A.C.P.," *Political Affairs*, XXIX (Feb., 1950), 26.
[20] *Ibid.*, p. 25.

strength where it did not exist or reverse the weakening of party influence in the Association.

How were the purposes of the NAACP leaders viewed? Strong gave the answer of the party hierarchy when he declared:

Negro businessmen, educators, physicians, lawyers, and social workers, though depending primarily upon a Negro market for their economic survival, are increasingly subjected to the ideological, political, and economic offensive of Wall Street. It is from this strata of the Negro population that the leadership of the N.A.A.C.P. has been historically drawn; it is primarily the interest of this group that the Wilkins-Current forces endeavor to represent and speak for. This wavering, petty-bourgeois leadership has set as its objective the subordination of the Negro people's liberation struggle to the . . . aims of American imperialism.[21]

Further, said Strong,

The Wilkins-Current leadership is working to build an all embracing reformist movement around the issue of civil rights legislation, inclusive of all Right-led unions, Social-Democrats, Trotskyites, and reactionary hierarchy-controlled Catholic organizations.

Gloster Current came in for special attack because as the NAACP's director of branches he had fought the Communists in many encounters. Moreover, he had beaten them. Wise to their ways and quietly firm, Current, with ample backing from the national office, never hesitated before the Stalinists in organizational fights. The party's latest attack on Current was a measure of his effectiveness in thwarting party designs on NAACP branches.

The viability of an organization like the NAACP is not bound up completely with its existing leaders. Although they man key posts and in the popular mind are inseparable from the

[21] *Ibid.*, p. 28.

institution, they are rarely indispensable. In attacking the NAACP leaders as it did, however, the party sought more than their removal from office. In effect, it proposed to eliminate the NAACP as an organization. For in the circumstances an overthrow of its leaders and adoption of the program advocated by the party would have sounded the death knell of the Association. The "Wilkins-Current leadership" was for the party only the first and most obvious target. Party domination of the NAACP, like its domination of other civil rights organizations, would have been a guarantee of the Association's demise. It is difficult to imagine that the Communists realistically anticipated or desired a different result.

They were restrained only by their own weakness and the strength of the opposition. So intent were they on building a Negro following that could be posed against American foreign policy that they would have regarded the NAACP in its entirety as a small sacrifice. The party's lack of resources and the dissolution of its Negro support, coupled with the resolution with which the NAACP and other indigenous groups were willing to meet the challenge, cut the ground from under any chances the party might otherwise have had to profit from Negro dissatisfaction during the past decade and a half. Reading the *Daily Worker*, especially in the postwar period, is like walking through a dream. Party pronouncements assumed the quality of ritualistic chants in which the uttering of words and the manipulation of sacred symbols were somehow equated with the transformation of reality.

It is true that there was unrest among colored folk in the United States after the war, but not of the kind the party desired. The American Negro of 1950 was not the same man he was in 1930, or even in 1940. Thousands of Negroes who had never been out of rural Alabama or Mississippi were suddenly drafted into the army in the early 1940's and sent to training camps all over the country and even overseas. Others moved to the North or West and found civilian jobs paying more money than they knew existed. Still others moved into southern cities, where they found a new way of living. Thus within a short period of time large numbers of colored Americans who had known virtually none of the advantages of urban civilization discovered telephones, radios, indoor toilets, supermarkets, decent schooling for their children, a regular cash income—and eventually television. In other words, they got a close-up look at some of the more attractive features of American life, and they wanted "in"—not merely for their great-grandchildren but for themselves, too.

In the postwar period legislation designed to help returning veterans enabled the ambitious young Negro to own his own home or farm, to learn a skilled craft, to set up in business, or even to get a college education; and he became increasingly impatient with segregation and prejudice which prevented full enjoyment of his new achievements. Even if he went North to escape discrimination, he found that racial prejudice is a national phenomenon. Resentment grew and festered, especially among the young.

Meanwhile the South itself was undergoing sharp economic change. Cattle now grazed in many fields that had once been white with cotton, as farms converted from row crops to grain and livestock. That shift plus mechanization of agriculture pushed white and colored workers off the land and into the cities. More and more southern towns heard the sound of factory whistles for the first time as industrialization grew apace. With more jobs and fewer people competing for them, incomes and living standards rose, even for colored folk.

In the general national prosperity of the postwar period, industry and its Madison Avenue consultants for the first time became aware of and eager to ingratiate themselves with the Negro as a consumer, and the Negro himself developed a growing awareness of his bargaining power in the market as a potential weapon in his struggle for equal rights. Where he attained the vote—in northern and in some southern cities (for example, Atlanta)—he also became increasingly cognizant of his bargaining power at the polls.

Protest is most likely to come not from those who have nothing but from those who have already acquired something. By the middle 1950's Negroes had acquired enough to want everything that full participation in American rights and privileges implies. They were ripe for new leadership, new plans, new methods. They did not find all they were looking for in the NAACP, which was pursuing the same ends with essentially the same means as in previous years. The dissatisfaction of the new breed of young Negroes was not with the NAACP's ends; the overwhelming majority of the young militants wanted to be a part of American society rather than to rearrange it fundamentally. Nor did they deny the importance of the NAACP's methods. What the NAACP was doing was necessary. But was it adequate?

By 1955 the Association had pushed the school desegregation cases through the Supreme Court and won a dramatic, seminal victory—on paper. A year passed, then two years, and though there was gratifying progress in some of the border states, most of the South dragged its feet or refused to budge. Would the NAACP have to take every local school board up the court hierarchy to the supreme tribunal of the land? How many millions of dollars—how many wasted years—would that take? Even after the final ruling in each case, how many paratroopers would the federal government have to send to a locality to enforce the decision? Meanwhile, how many new generations of Negro children would have grown up with second-class schooling and second-class citizenship? Was the end result of all the NAACP's efforts the "integration" of a handful of hand-picked colored children in white schools, as at Little Rock or Charlotte? Furthermore, what about other kinds of segregation: in public parks, in libraries, in hotels, in restaurants, on buses and trains, and so on?

Such questions as these and a search for more effective methods produced the Montgomery and Tuskegee boycotts, the freedom rides, the sit-ins, and other nonviolent, direct-action techniques as supplementary weapons to the more strictly legalistic approach of the NAACP. The new methods were pioneered and developed in the churches and in the colleges, largely outside the NAACP. They caught on fast, spreading from locality to locality spontaneously as their successes were publicized.

It was not that the NAACP had not increased its own militancy in the postwar period. It had adopted a slogan of full civil rights by 1963, the centennial of Lincoln's Emancipation Proclamation. It had broadened its target to include that most sacrosanct and sensitive of Jim Crow institutions, the public school. It is one thing to ask admission of Negroes to graduate schools at the University of Maryland; it is quite another to insist on admission to grammar schools in Jackson, Mississippi. But whereas the Association had begun to attack discrimination at its very roots; whereas it pressed militantly for full rights in housing, education, recreation, and all other areas; whereas it sponsored some demonstrations, mass meetings, and marches, its main reliance was on judicial procedures, painstaking prosecution of its cause through the courts.

The Negro community was not a monolith. There were some who thought the NAACP was trying to go too fast. Many of the business and professional leaders, who had always constituted the core of the NAACP's membership, were in favor of a more virile prosecution of discrimination through legal procedures but felt uneasy at, if not horrified by, the first experiments of college students with the sit-in. They had been slow to realize that changes in the white community had made direct-action techniques by Negroes feasible for the first time.

The war had expanded the horizons of many white southerners. Industrialization had created a growing middle class whose members were as eager to enjoy suburbia without controversy as were their northern counterparts. A larger group of "responsible" white folk—businessmen and industrialists—now had an equity in the preservation of racial peace so as to attract even more industry to the South. The ranks of illiterate "rednecks" who were willing to take the law into their own hands and wreak violence on "uppity niggers" were thinning. The "new way" was to use economic rather than physical coercion. True, here and there violence erupted; but the salient aspect of the postwar struggle for civil rights, given the new militancy of the Negro, was not how much but how little actual violence occurred. The young college Negro had correctly sensed that if he sat down on a lunch counter stool or in a public library in his neatly pressed suit and refused in a courteous, cultured voice to leave until he was served, the middle-class white southerner, particularly in the cities, would take a dim view of any illiterate "wool-hat" who tried to bash his head in. A combination of deep-seated guilt plus growing absorption with non-racial matters among white southerners help to explain the successes of the boycotts and sit-ins.

It is important to evaluate the activities of the NAACP in the postwar period in the light of the temper of the times. Since racialism runs deep in the historical tradition of America, permeating American institutions, the realization of NAACP goals would bring a drastic transformation in the national social structure. But the "revolution" moved under the banner of law and order. It was waged in the name of America's loftiest ideals, which have been in conflict with its practices. A growing number of white Americans have endorsed the NAACP's aims, and the Association's opponents have been put ever more on the defensive, even in the South. So respectable have civil rights become that every President since Franklin

Roosevelt has pledged himself to reduce discrimination. Even die-hard Mississippians have come to realize that it is only a matter of time, that what they are fighting is a delaying action rather than a decisive battle. Perhaps Harry Ashmore's *Epitaph for Dixie* points the way to a second Appomattox.

It is in this context that the postwar militancy of the NAACP and other racial groups must be seen. The demands the Association has made and the accomplishments it has achieved are not novel in kind, but the degree of success is in marked contrast with the prewar period. Its goals have not changed, but they have sharpened; and its timetable has been greatly revised. There was a time when its immediate goal was to get southern states to live up to the "separate but equal" school laws; now it demands not that segregated schools be equalized but that they be abolished. No longer does it petition employers to provide Negroes with jobs of any sort; it demands that Negroes be hired and promoted on the basis of ability. Nor is it satisfied with crumbs from the political tables; it insists on a full-course dinner and uses the voting power of Negroes to get access to the menu—all this, not in the name of a revolutionary new social order, but in the name of equalitarian promises which form the very fabric of the old order. The cry is not "something" but "more." If this is revolution, it is not the revolution that the Communists have envisioned. For, if successful, it will strengthen the bourgeois order and the American middle-class ideology, enabling one-tenth of the citizenry previously excluded to live in tract houses, wear grey flannel suits, shop in the supermarkets, and achieve "togetherness."

Significantly, it may well have been the very aggressiveness of the NAACP, rather than its alleged conservatism, that led to the loss of some of its followers after 1950. Like most whites in the South, some Negroes felt that the NAACP tried to move "too far too fast." A small number of Negroes no doubt were honestly convinced that the charge that the Association was Communist or Communist-influenced was true. A handful of Negro professional anti-Communists, mostly ex-Communists, in newspaper articles and before investigating committees made their standard charges against the Association. Their testimony was eagerly seized upon by southern politicians and right-wing editors who wanted to impede the NAACP's progress by painting the Association with a red brush.

For conservative whites it became more and more difficult to find reliable "Nigrahs," even in the South, who would denounce the NAACP and tell whites what they longed to hear about Yankee radicals at the helm of the organization. The great majority of Negroes, even those in such out-of-the-way places as Hylan Lewis' "Kent," knew that although it might be inexpedient for them to belong to the NAACP, they could not justify their reluctance on grounds that the organization was "Red." They suspected, and their prior experience, supported this view, that the charge was intended to screen segregationist efforts to defeat demands for racial justice. If such Negroes could not argue the facts and principles with the white man in the open, they could and did applaud the NAACP's efforts in secret; and they participated in those efforts vicariously if not overtly. Indeed, when the time came for them to stand up and be counted, many displayed a fortitude that must have been surprising, even to themselves. It takes courage for a Negro bank janitor in Kingtree, South Carolina, to sign a petition to the local school asking that his child be enrolled in the white grade school—especially if the bank threatens to foreclose the mortgage on his home if he signs the petition.

Like many other American citizens in the early 1950's some Negroes abstained from support of the NAACP because of that phenomenon which has come to be characterized as "McCarthyism." Aware that Communist influence was never substantial in the Association, they were nonetheless frightened by the charge and chose to play it safe. Particularly was this the case among government workers and those who anticipated making careers in the civil service. They feared, with some justification, that membership in the NAACP might have an adverse effect on their employment chances and promotion opportunities.

Needless to say, leaders of the Association were disturbed by that development. In principle they had reservations about the many practices of government agencies, legislative and administrative, which inquired into the political preferences of individual citizens. Moreover, as officers of a voluntary protest organization, they were concerned about the implications of such activities for the membership growth and effectiveness of the Association. The amount of time and energy that the NAACP staff used in countering misgivings among prospective members and in defending individual members against specific charges was, as one NAACP officer said in an interview, "a real drain on us personally and a big handicap in trying to recruit members." That time and energy could have been used for other purposes.

Toward the end of the 1950's there was some decline in the anti-Communist hysteria; the laws of diminishing returns began to operate in political witch-hunting. From that turn of events the NAACP benefited, for it could thenceforth concentrate more forcefully on an affirmative program, despite the fact that in the early 1960's there came a resurgent right-wing anticommunism which, though in many instances not overtly racist, has enlisted in its ranks some of the nation's most vociferous proponents of white supremacy, including United States Senators who have no love for the NAACP.

During the McCarthy era the Communists attempted to approach the NAACP on a we're-all-in-this-thing-together basis. The Association, however, would have none of that; both

Walter White and Roy Wilkins, who succeeded him as executive secretary, went to great lengths to make the organization's position clear. They asserted that NAACP refusal to
participate jointly with Communist (and suspected Communist) organizations in joint efforts to protect the political rights
of individuals and groups before government agencies and
among the general public was informed by previous experiences with such cooperation, in which the Communists' sometime concern with the basic principles involved had been
clearly demonstrated.

It was during the McCarthy era that the Communists again
became momentarily introspective about their Negro program
and about the role of Negroes in the party itself. This did
not occur until they found themselves in real difficulty, with
their influence among Negroes declining rapidly and with
non-Communist Negro organizations combating and isolating
party members when the opportunity arose. When the party
faithful finally asked, "What is wrong with us in relation to
the Negro?" they sought the answers with a self-flagellation
that paralleled the soul-searching of the early postwar years.

Toward the middle of the 1950's the Communists subjected
their Negro program to another review, a move prompted by
their inability to hold on to Negro members or to attract new
ones to the ranks. The party's self-estimate was best expressed
in a revealing series of articles in *Political Affairs* in 1953 and
1954.

One article in particular pinpointed what the Communists
considered the basic weaknesses in their Negro work. It began
with the usual assertion that the party had been in the forefront of the Negro liberation struggles of the past and had
played a vital role in the postwar period following reorganization of the party and elimination of the reformist influences
of the deposed Browder. It was conceded, however, that the
party might have done much more in the field of race relations

had its members understood more clearly the basic theoretical approach of the party and been more aware of certain broad social developments which were important to the Negro question.

In engaging in Negro work, the Communists, it was claimed, were faulty in not appreciating the basic significance of the "national character" of the Negro question; that is, they had not taken seriously and sought to apply in day-to-day activities the slogan of self-determination for Negroes in the Black Belt which was reinstituted shortly after the war. Second, it was argued, party members had themselves been guilty of racial prejudice, which found expression within the organization and hampered work with Negroes. Party members also had a tendency to accept the tenet of gradualism, which led them to a false estimate of the possibilities of "bourgeois nationalist" organizations such as the NAACP. Further, Communists had been both too pessimistic and too optimistic in gauging broader racial developments. They underestimated the volume and intensity of discontent among Negroes, particularly the middle class, and the possibilities this offered for development of large-scale racial movements. At the same time they had taken much too rosy a view of the labor unions, assuming that discrimination could be eliminated and the groundwork laid for Negro-labor unity, about which there had been so much talk and for which there had been such hope.[22]

The party's defection could be overcome, it was argued, by several steps that would produce "theoretical clarity" and organizational effectiveness in "Negro work." The first step was to popularize the Marxist theoretical and political program on the Negro question. That was to be followed by development of an "action agenda" on racial discrimination "in all

[22] Samuel T. Henderson, "White Chauvinism and Negro Bourgeois Nationalism" (I), *Political Affairs*, XXXI (Dec., 1952), *passim*.

phases of [Negro] life," the organization of cadres "of thousands" who would be able to go into

any county, any section, any club of the Party and successfully carry through and organize the struggle against white chauvinism and the struggle for a program of mass action in the fight for Negro rights, without at all times having to have the participation of the highest committees of the Party,

and finally, the "merging of this inner-Party struggle with the mass struggle for Negro rights on the basis of united front action of every type." [23]

The author admitted that many obstacles stood in the way of applying the remedies. First, there was resistance in the CP itself to concentrating on the Negro question. Second, "many of our white comrades . . . fail to pose the struggle for Negro rights in its connection and relationship to the general problems of the mass of white workers and to the current assaults upon the foreign-born." Third, "too few of our white leaders . . . are equipped to estimate current trends" among the Negro people; "too many fail to keep up with these developments and have to get any estimate of trends in the Negro movement second-hand." Fourth, there were still "strong paternalistic tendencies [in the Party] reflecting a petty bourgeois orientation, on the part of many of our white cadres." Finally, among some members "there [was] a hypercritical attitude toward Negro leadership," especially among Communists in trade-unions.

Since these were internal obstacles, they could, it was argued, be overcome if members understood and combated them effectively. The real enemy was external, bourgeois Negro nationalism. The Negro middle class and its organizations, the party theorized, were committed to gradualism,

[23] Henderson, "White Chauvinism" (II), *passim.*

expressed most crudely in the appeal to bourgeois humanitarianism "We are American too," which was the plaintive call of a weak bourgeoisie to the white ruling class to [obtain] that which can be accomplished only by the combined struggles of a broad people's coalition of Negroes, white farmers and urban middle classes led by the working class against the white monopoly capitalists.

This analysis contained several admissions; the most notable related to intraparty race relations. Of almost equal significance was the recognition of the ineffectiveness of the party's appeal to Negroes generally. The castigation of the "bourgeois Negro nationalists" was not unexpected in view of the fact that the party had long regarded them and the NAACP, which was under their leadership, as the principal ideological and organizational roadblocks in the race field. Although these observations indicated a close touch with reality, the belief that the party could overcome the obstacles with the instruments proposed had once more an ethereal quality.

It was insisted further that

from the point of view of Marxism, Negro bourgeois nationalism is reactionary. Proletarian internationalism and Negro bourgeois nationalism are irreconcilable ideologies. They are in conflict, and either one or the other must triumph. They cannot exist side by side.

The Communists admitted that the colored middle class might have a role to play, up to a point. But beyond that the Negro *bourgeoisie* would not go and could not be expected to go. In this view the middle class could be used by the Communists and ought to be used as long as it served their purposes; in the end, however, it would have to be eliminated, swept away by the inevitable forces of history working through the proletariat. In the interim the comrades proposed to work with

197

the "Cadillac crowd," attempting to steer it on the proper course, but always remembering that true Communists must turn against the black *bourgeoisie* when their usefulness was done with. For the present the Communists felt they

needed among our leading Negro cadre . . . a very conscious mobilization to fight to carry out the line of the Party, to work with the masses in the Right-led, reformist organizations and, in the first place, the N.A.A.C.P. It is only in this way that the program of the Party can be brought into line and result in the development of mass united front action in the struggle for Negro rights.[24]

The Association's leaders, of course, had long recognized that the party would use the organization where it could and then attack it if the situation changed. They knew, too (it had been demonstrated time and again and in this instance it was admitted forthrightly by the CP) that the aims of the two groups were basically incompatible. The structural and functional differences, the polarized ideologies and strategies, and the conflicting definitions of means and ends had never been sharper. It was in the light of these and similar pronouncements by Communist functionaries that the NAACP viewed the offers of "cooperation," the calls for "unity," the pleas for a "united front." Like other non-Communist Negro leaders, those in the Association were not likely to embark on joint measures with the party, even if Senators from Mississippi saw no difference between the two organizations. The NAACP, of course, would have been more disturbed had there been much likelihood that the Communists could implement their declared intentions. But that was a danger neither clear nor present.

[24] *Ibid.* For a restatement of the over-all CP analysis and approach on the Negro question in the post-Korean War era, see William Z. Foster, "Left Sectarianism in the Fight for Negro Rights and against White Chauvinism," *Political Affairs*, XXXII (June, 1953), 17–31.

The party's deteriorating position among Negroes was further reflected in the third convention of the National Negro Labor Council, which met in Chicago in December, 1953. Between the second and third meetings the council had been placed on the Attorney General's subversive list and additionally handicapped by the fight waged against it by the NAACP and anti-Communist Negro and white trade-union leaders. Party spokesmen noted that there was considerable doubt, even in their own ranks, about the desirability of such an organization as the NNLC; those who should have supported it with enthusiasm were in many instances merely "tipping their hats" in its direction. Perhaps some non-Communists might have been drawn into the NNLC had they not found in the NAACP a more effective organization, broader in scope and able to get things done. Even the comrades conceded that the NAACP was "the most important organization of the Negro people, and on many fronts has done a very good job," though "the leadership of the NAACP is petty bourgeois leadership and by itself and of itself cannot wage a consistent struggle along the lines that we are indicating." Both organizations (NAACP and NNLC), it was held, should be supported, but the limits of the former should always be borne in mind.[25]

The 1953 meeting of the NNLC, with less than half as many delegates as attended the first convention, signaled the end of the short, unhappy life of the party's major organization among Negro workers in the postwar period. For the NNLC's collapse the NAACP and particularly its labor secretary, Herbert Hill, could claim a certain credit. Since the NNLC's inception the NAACP had campaigned against it within those unions with substantial Negro memberships, from which the NNLC tried to draw followers.[26]

[25] Pettis Perry, "The Third Annual Convention of the National Negro Labor Council," *Political Affairs*, XXXIII (Feb., 1954), 3.
[26] NAACP, *Labor Manual*, p. 70.

Contributing also to the decline of the NNLC were the labor organizations themselves, particularly the CIO, a number of whose affiliates, frequently prodded by the NAACP, established internal antidiscrimination committees. The most notable were those in the United Automobile Workers and the United Packinghouse Workers unions.[27] Although the committees in other unions were less effective, they did serve as useful instruments for resolving grievances based on race. Where the committees brought about even modest changes in union and industry practices, Negro members felt it unnecessary to invoke the assistance of the NNLC or other outside, politically oriented organizations. When they did seek outside help, it was usually from the NAACP.

All too frequently, however, the national as well as the local union committees were manned by incompetent people, as mediocre Negroes received appointments in return for political support of white officers. From a union's internal view, the Negro committeemen symbolized the interracial equality of the organization and suggested participation of Negroes in the top-level decision-making process, but what sociologists would term their "latent" functions were significantly different from the "manifest" ones.

Some committees, in fact, suppressed intraunion racial unrest and tried to modulate the sharp cries against discrimination by seriously aggrieved Negro members. Some regarded their principal function as public relations, in which they sought to convey to liberal critics an image of the union as a stronghold of racial equality. Protecting the top leaders from charges of prejudice or of inaction on racial issues in the union and the industry was another task they performed. The ineffectiveness of some of the committees and the absence of such committees altogether in a number of the AFL-CIO affili-

[27] John Hope II, *Equality of Opportunity* (Washington: Public Affairs Press, 1956); Howe and Widick, *op. cit.*, pp. 226–227.

ates later led A. Philip Randolph to organize the American Negro Labor Council to advance race rights in the labor movement. For the NAACP the committees were important because they were official instruments through which its concerns could often be expressed and through which Communist efforts among Negro union members might be opposed.

By 1954 the party was in such a precarious position that it renewed efforts to work through the NAACP. At its 1953 convention the Association had adopted the slogan, "Free by Sixty-Three," expressing the determination to secure full citizenship for Negroes by the hundredth anniversary of the Emancipation Proclamation. "Left-sectarians" in the party criticized the Association for offering the hope that through legislative and judicial means Negroes could reach the goal. However, higher-ranking Communists concluded that such a slogan should not be dismissed lightly. The party, they said, should exploit the enthusiasm the slogan would produce among Association members and Negroes generally. Limitations of the NAACP's program were to be shown to the "Negro masses," however, and conditions for attainment of "real freedom" propounded. "Real freedom," the party insisted, included the right of self-determination for Negroes in the Black Belt, and its realization required fundamental alteration of the social and economic structure of the southern region. If the NAACP's slogan was understood to mean the end of segregation and discrimination, it

must be fought for [by Communists] and in fighting for it [they must] thereby . . . help move it from integrationist by-ways into the path of struggle for Negro liberation. It is only in this way that the shortcomings of the middle-class Negro leaders can be overcome and the struggle for real freedom of the Negro people advanced.[28]

[28] Abner W. Berry, "On the Slogan 'Free by 63,'" *Political Affairs,* XXXIII (Feb., 1954), 14.

Communists were to use the opportunity even if they had to endorse a call to action which the Association had originated and popularized. Party support, even though not invited, was offered only as a ruse for taking the ball from the NAACP and running with it toward a goal that was never marked by the original "Free by Sixty-Three" slogan.

The NAACP, of course, was eager to secure support for the slogan's many objectives and to turn the enthusiasm of Negroes to organized account. But it did not seek and did not want help from the Communist Party and its race organizations. Party members, whose tactical training included close examination of Lenin's sacred commentaries on slogans as devices for arousing and directing the masses, could not have failed to be chagrined that the Association rather than the comrades had coined such a ringing phrase, one that struck such a responsive chord among Negroes.

After seeing the NAACP use the "Free by Sixty-Three" slogan effectively in membership and fund-raising drives and in appeals to other Negro organizations, the Communists were less open in their disparagement and in their intentions to manipulate the slogan to their own advantage. However, they continued their attacks on the NAACP and its leaders, although they were less inclined to name names. And they held out the possibility that even benighted reformists in race organizations were not altogether hopeless. Said one high-ranking party spokesman:

There exists the danger coming from a section of the Negro reformers and misleaders. It would be wrong to say, however, that all the Negro reformers and all the Negro bourgeoisie no longer are capable of making a contribution to the Negro liberation movement. The Negro liberation movement is an all-class movement. But to be effective the Negro workers, who are part of the working class of this country, must be more and more brought to the fore in this titanic struggle. This does not mean, however, that every possible force among the petty bourgeois and bourgeois elements among the Negroes that can be worked with in alliance to further the liberation effort should be neglected.[29]

In indicating the specific alliances to be formed with Negro "bourgeois elements," the official significantly found few individuals or organizations to whom the Communists might turn. He was especially disturbed by the fact that no NAACP leaders sought to prevent the "outlawing" of the Communist Party and that some of them, including Benjamin Mays, had suggested that its official proscription might be a desirable step. If the Association and other Negro organizations would not fight for the legal status of the party, they were not likely to form alliances with it.

In the spring of 1954 the Communists' Negro program received a further setback and the NAACP's approach a tremendous boost by the Supreme Court decision which held that racially segregated public schools were unconstitutional. The implications of that decision and of the implementary ruling made a year later were far-reaching, affecting the entire nation's political, social, and educational structures and bringing to the surface racial tensions that had been relatively submerged. Much has been and will be written about the court's action, and for many years to come political conflicts, especially in the South, will center on efforts to abide by or to resist the court's mandate. The concern here is only with a very limited aspect of the high tribunal's ruling—its impact on relations between the NAACP and the Communist Party.

In the public's mind the laurel wreath was placed on the NAACP's brow, for the Association had sparked the fight, pushing through the courts the cases on which the great break-

[29] Pettis Perry, "The Negro People in the Struggle against McCarthyism" (Draft-Program Discussion), *Political Affairs*, XXXIII (May, 1954), 40.

through came. Indeed, the school cases were but the culmination of a whole series of litigations which, over the years, hacked away at the legal underpinnings of segregation—in voting, transportation, employment, and so on. The cases were prepared with habitual thoroughness that could but evoke the grudging admiration of even the most die-hard segregationist; and they were argued with characteristic brilliance by the NAACP's legal staff, headed by Thurgood Marshall. The unanimous decisions of 1954–1955 supporting educational integration were dramatic evidence that the labors of the NAACP had not been in vain, that its techniques could pay dividends.

Among Negroes all over the country and even in the white community the prestige of the Association soared. It had challenged successfully not only the moral grounds of white supremacy but also the very institutional structures through which it was sustained. Because the NAACP had placed so much emphasis on the courts as instruments for racial change, its leaders underestimated the limits of legal devices as instruments for modifying basic attitudes and established institutionalized practices. They would have done well to recall what happened (or didn't happen) in the wake of the initial nullification of the white primary in the 1920's.

The victory was a legal one, and realization of its substance was not to come about automatically. To implement the decisions the Association had to develop specific challenges to local and state agencies in the southern and border states. Rarely was it able to achieve voluntary compliance; that circumstance placed upon local branches—and the parents and children of colored southerners—the onus of progress. The segregationists would employ every legal, and sometimes illegal, means to delay the bright harvest. A measure of the effectiveness and determination of the NAACP was found in the extremes to which southern white groups—official, semi-official, and private—went in attempts to "outlaw" the Association. It was assumed that since the NAACP, and not the "happy Nigrahs," was responsible for the decision in the first place, its destruction would automatically lead to the *status quo ante* in southern education.

The Communists may well have hoped that the court would rule against the plaintiffs in the school cases and continue legal sanctions of racial segregation. Such a decision would have done immeasurable damage to the NAACP, and the party could have proclaimed with some substance the futility of legalistic methods, the unreliability of the judiciary in providing racial justice, and the emptiness of Negro hopes of securing full citizenship through instruments acceptable to a bourgeois society.

Of course, the party could scarcely have voiced its reservations about the courts publicly; indeed, one of its leading spokesmen rushed in to say that the court—the same dastardly court that refused to reverse the Dennis ruling—had "struck a mighty blow at the entire system of racial segregation in our country." [30] But then he went on to ask, "How does it happen that this momentous democratic victory is won from the High Court of U. S. Imperialism precisely when the monopoly ruling class is stepping up its reactionary drive to fascism and war?" [31] What the court had really done, he concluded, "was to bow to the increased power of the Negro people and their democratic, peace-loving allies in our country and throughout the world." Further, he said, "within the complex of progressive developments responsible for the outlawing of segregated schools, the major cause was the unity and militancy in the struggle of the Negro masses and their leaders in the N.A.A.C.P." [32] This concession must have come hard, for the party only a short time before had jeered the NAACP's legal

---

[30] Doxey A. Wilkerson, "The Fight to Abolish Segregated Schools," *Political Affairs*, XXXIII (July, 1954), 29.

[31] *Ibid.*   [32] *Ibid.*, p. 34.

strategy and had castigated its leaders for partiality toward the Negro middle class and neglect of the black masses. In the circumstances, however, it had little choice. It could hardly afford not to approve of the ruling and not to applaud the organization chiefly responsible for it.

Somehow the Communists managed to interpret the school segregation victories of the NAACP as the "key role of the Negro nation in the struggle for Negro liberation," claiming that the "fight for equality of educational opportunity was initiated by Negro working class and agrarian masses in the Black Belt." [33] (The same spokesman, a few years before in an intraparty debate on self-determination, had argued that there was no such thing as a Negro nation in the South and that the theory of self-determination was inapplicable to the historical experience, institutional structure, and authentic aspirations of Negroes.) Only by ignoring the facts that the suits had been instituted by the NAACP through its national office, fought with funds supplied in large measure by Negroes outside the South, and involved Negro parents and children who themselves were primarily middle class could the party make this claim. However, some explanation or official pronouncement was mandatory, particularly for Negroes in the Communist ranks who, however "reliable," could not help but compare the solid achievements of the NAACP with the meager, side-line role of the party in this momentous episode.

Soaring even higher above reality, the party asserted that the "Negro workers are the main dynamic force, ever pressing for new gains in the fight for democratic rights," although the state of "working class hegemony over the Negro liberation movement" had not yet been achieved. It was conceded that the NAACP "mobilized the best professional talent in the land for effective argument in the courts, and rallied the whole

[33] *Ibid.*, p. 36.

Negro people, together with their allies, in powerful support."
Without any aid from the party—in fact, rejecting the Communists' prior calls for cooperation and unity—the NAACP had
been able to grasp an objective the party thought unreachable.
The CP's response was to read into the tea leaves of history its
own wishes.

Frantically trying, after the curtain was lowered, to create
for itself at least a peripheral role in the great racial drama, it
proclaimed that

the vanguard role of the Communist Party in many past struggles
for Negro rights has contributed markedly to the unity and
militancy of the Negro liberation movement, and has helped to
win important allies for the Negro people. Further, the struggles
of our Party against fascism and war have done much to strengthen
the broad people's movement for democracy and peace, and
thus to help wrest Negro-rights concessions from our war-
bound imperialist government. Even so, the fact remains that,
aside from the activities of individual Communists unspecified
here and there, our Party played no direct role in the fight to
outlaw segregated schools.[34]

The Communist Party had declared repeatedly that it welcomed characterization as a "racial equality" and "Negro
rights" organization. Now it admitted that it had been on the
side lines while one of the most seminal battles in a half century
of Negro struggles had been fought. The party of the "Negro
masses" conceded that it was guilty of "strong and widespread
negative attitudes toward struggles led by the petty bourgeoisie coupled with overestimation of the present state in the
development of the leading role of Negro workers." It ac-
knowledged that it had misgauged the "political significance
of the fight against segregated schools, probably stemming in
part from our general tendency to neglect issues in the field of

[34] *Ibid.*, p. 42.

education," and had isolated its Negro cadres from "the mass organizations of the Negro people." [35]

The court's decision was a great blow to the Communist Party as it was a triumph for the NAACP. A few months later, however, when the shock had worn off, the party recovered its poise. The court's decision, it then said, merely confirmed its earlier analysis of the Negro question. The change of mind was echoed in a subsequent CP declaration:

The Supreme Court decision on segregation in education reflects the tremendous new growth in the Negro liberation movement. This victory likewise is due to the increased support of a broad section of the white population, particularly the labor movement. It is due further to the growth of the colonial liberation movements and their powerful impact upon the events in our country. It is due in no small part to the pioneering role of the Communists and Left in the struggle for Negro rights.[36]

Then, grasping the full impact of the ruling and searching for ways to become involved in the NAACP's efforts to implement it, the Communists altered their tactics sharply. They called for legislation outlawing discrimination in employment, housing, and education; they offered to support political candidates without insisting on acceptance of other items on the Communist agenda. They wanted cooperation of all segments of the Negro community and the "unity of the Negro people" on terms other than those on which Communists had previously insisted. Particularly did the Communists hope that Negro-labor unity might be achieved, for that would give them an opportunity to work more effectively, in the South in particular.[37] This ostensible dropping of its "sectarian" pose, it

[35] "Draft Program of the Communist Party on the Negro Question," quoted in *ibid.*, p. 43.

[36] Pettis Perry, "The November Elections and the Struggle for Jobs, Peace, Equal Rights, and Democracy," *Political Affairs*, XXXIII (Sept. 1954), 32.

[37] *Ibid., passim.*

is now clear, was an act of desperation in an effort to involve the party in what, obviously, would be the main arenas of racial conflict in the United States for a great many years ahead.

The party, however, was by then even further isolated from both labor and racial movements. Chances that it could make any effective alliances with either declined with each passing day. Even had Communists been acceptable to such organizations as the NAACP or the political arms of the AFL-CIO, they could have contributed only very limited resources to an alliance. When the party talked for internal consumption, it scourged its members for having lost touch with Negro and labor groups; when it talked for public ears, it bragged about its influence with the white and colored masses.

In offering its help in the school desegregation struggles, the party was guided by still another concern. A consideration of its concern requires further reference to "McCarthyism" and the loyalty security programs of the government during the mid-1950's. At its forty-fourth convention in 1953 the NAACP had expressed unease about the growing denial of due process and adequate representation for individuals accused before congressional committees and loyalty boards of being subversives. Noting particularly the use of expressed beliefs in racial equality and association of Negroes and whites on an equal basis socially as an index of radicalism, or at least as a source of suspicion, the NAACP was understandably disturbed. It pointed out that belief in the individual worth and equality of human beings did not make one an agent of the Kremlin. It concluded by calling upon "all our people to stand firm upon the platform of the Americanism of the founding fathers." [38] Communists made much of the Association's concern for civil liberties, stating that "the clear principles

[38] NAACP, *The Year of the Great Decision: NAACP Annual Report,* 1954 (New York: NAACP, 1954), p. 71.

enunciated in the resolution provide the basis for the widest participation of all democratic forces in a struggle which will not only check, but rout McCarthyism." [39] They failed to mention that the same NAACP convention reiterated its opposition to the party and reaffirmed its intention of keeping party members out of the NAACP, even if this required expulsion of branches which fell under CP control.

Furthermore, the NAACP would have none of the party-sponsored Committee to Defend Negro Leadership (CDNL), an organization established to raise funds and provide legal and propaganda aid to colored Communists who were hailed before immigration boards, congressional committees, or loyalty panels, and in some instances indicted and tried in the courts. Walter White, while expressing doubts about the procedures of many government agencies generally and condemning some of them specifically, labeled the CDNL a "Communist front" and rejected flatly its invitation to him and to other NAACP leaders to serve as members or sponsors.

That government agencies were sometimes used to attack individuals because they were leaders of Negro protest (as in the case of Ralph Bunche), not because they were Communists or even alleged Communists, posed a real dilemma for the NAACP. Moreover, there was the question of whether a civil rights organization ought not to defend Communists, Negro or white, on the basis of its fundamental commitment. The position of the NAACP, like that of many other action organizations, was ambivalent; confusion and hesitancy were apparent in a declaration of general principles that was coupled with a disposition to intervene only when there was reasonable certainty that the individual or organization was not Communist and by a prohibition of Communist membership in its own organization on the grounds that party members were either subversives

[39] Frederick C. Hastings, "Unite the Negro People against McCarthyism," *Political Affairs*, XXXIII (Oct., 1954), 37.

or foreign agents or both. The dilemma was real, and not one of the NAACP officials who were interviewed during the mid-1950's was entirely comfortable with the organization's action at the 1953 convention and afterward.

For their refusal to participate in the Committee to Defend Negro Leadership, for pointing to its origins and composition, and for their ambivalent position on "McCarthyism," White and the NAACP were bitterly attacked by the Communists. Particularly were they castigated for not coming to the defense of Benjamin Davis, Henry Winston, Ferdinand Smith, Paul Robeson, W. E. B. Du Bois, and other Negroes who had become closely identified either with the party or with organizations under its control.[40] In sum, the party held that the "policy now of Walter White with his 'loyalty standards' can only extend to other Negro Leaders the whiplash of McCarthyism. Mr. White's policies must be rejected by the mass intervention of the membership of the NAACP." [41] Such intervention was not forthcoming; one reason was that there existed no substantial sentiment among NAACP members for aiding people who had, over the years and even quite recently, sought to destroy the Association. Even had there been widespread sympathy for the Communists among the NAACP's rank and file, the feeling would have been difficult to express in the absence of concurrence on the part of the national staff and the Executive Board.

The NAACP and its leaders were attacked as "Communist" even more intensively following the Supreme Court's school segregation decision. Such attacks stemmed chiefly from the NAACP's involvement in the school desegregation process and came from sources whose motivations were patent. One can only conjecture about whether the assaults would have been fewer and less vehement if the Association had taken and implemented a more forthright position against McCarthyism.

[40] *Ibid.*, pp. 39–43.   [41] *Ibid.*

To have defended Negro Communists—and Stalinists in general—insofar as their basic civil rights were being violated would have been a risky business for the Association, caught as it already was in the propaganda cross fire of racial bigotry North and South. In the general hysteria, NAACP leaders would have been hard put to convince even some of the Association's natural friends that it was defending the right of political dissent rather than treason.

Significantly, the accusation of "communism" was hurled at the NAACP at the very time when McCarthyism was losing its force and when the once relatively strong Communist movement was declining at an accelerating pace. Even though strong approval of the Association was voiced by many prominent public figures, their words were not heeded by its critics.[42] The House Committee on Un-American Activities labeled the NAACP "a non-Communist organization" and conceded that the party had made little headway among Negroes. In a report released in late 1954 the committee stated:

From the facts set forth in this report, the committee can only conclude that the vast majority of Americans of the Negro race have consistently resisted the blandishments and treacherous promises offered them by the Communist conspirators. The committee hopes that this detailed exposure of the true Communist aims and tactics in relation to the Negro people will serve even further to reduce the extremely limited and temporary Negro support which the Communists have obtained by subterfuge.[43]

The southern state legislative and administrative committees —in Arkansas, Florida, Alabama, and Louisiana—then provided official platforms from which "expert witnesses," a number of them imported from north of the Mason-Dixon line and some of them former Communists, could charge the NAACP

[42] NAACP, *NAACP Acclaimed by Distinguished Americans* (New York: NAACP, 1956).
[43] *Amer. Negro in CP.*

with being Communist and its officers with having been affiliated with organizations that were radical or subversive if not altogether "Red." Few readers can examine the transcripts of the hearings without sensing how eager the investigators were to daub the NAACP with the red brush and how few reservations they had about the means for doing it. Such investigations, widely publicized, were among the responses of the white South's officialdom to the school segregation decisions. They were conceived as one means of discrediting, and in some cases "outlawing," the organization chiefly responsible for the Supreme Court rulings and totally dedicated to enforcing them.[44]

When the party took stock of itself on the race issue in 1955, it admitted it was being increasingly isolated from Negroes and their organizations; but in characteristic fashion it went on to claim that it had considerable influence and a reservoir of "good will" based on its previous "contributions to the case of Negro freedom." [45] The influence, however, had "not kept pace with the rapid growth and development of the Negro people's freedom movement itself," with the result that "a dangerous gap exists between these two, which, if not narrowed, can have the most harmful consequences for the cause of Negro freedom, for democracy and progress." [46] Again, the main culprit was the "persistence of strong sectarian tendencies which tend to isolate our Party from many of the movements, organizations and struggles engaged in by the majority of the Negro people." [47] The answer, claimed an article in *Political Affairs,* was a "mass policy" in the field of Negro

[44] Joint Legislative Committee, State of Louisiana, *Subversion in Racial Unrest: An Outline of a Strategic Weapon to Destroy the Governments of Louisiana and the United States* (Baton Rouge: State of Louisiana, 1957).

[45] Frederick C. Hastings and Charles P. Mann, "For a Mass Policy in Negro Freedom's Cause," *Political Affairs,* XXXIV (March, 1955), 7.

[46] *Ibid.*   [47] *Ibid.*

213

work. How to develop such a policy was the question. Again, the central position of the NAACP was recognized: "The N.A.A.C.P. is viewed by the Negro people as their own organized mass weapon which has won many important battles for them in recent years." But, it was asked, "If the Negro people have transformed the N.A.A.C.P. into a mass organization of struggle very much different from what it was in the '30s how can we reconcile this fact with the character of the N.A.A.C.P. leadership?" [48]

Admittedly, the NAACP leaders had not changed basically; they remained what they had always been: "reformist supporters of the white ruling class," who retained their positions only by responding, albeit reluctantly, to the needs of working-class Negroes. Had there been no such response, the article claimed, "the initiative and leadership exercised by the Communists and Left Progressives would have resulted in the whole Negro liberation movement being organized and led by the working-class ideology and leadership of our Party." [49] The backhanded compliment to the flexibility of the NAACP leaders and the grudging concession that they had been successful was another way of saying that Negroes had been attracted to a reformist, pragmatic program and had rejected the doctrinaire alternative offered by the party. It was an admission, too, that the NAACP had cut the ground from under the Communists by demonstrating the workability of moderate racial movements in a political community that still permitted generally, if not in Alabama, a relatively wide range of protest and pressure.

One may speculate, as did the Communists, that lower-strata Negroes would have turned to the party if more gradualist programs had failed and if the NAACP had been crushed. It does not seem likely, however, that this would have occurred. The party's claim rested on the assumption that the more deprived and downtrodden a people, the greater will be their revolu-

[48] *Ibid.*, p. 11.   [49] *Ibid.*

tionary unrest. The unrestful, articulate Negroes in the 1930's and since, however, have been chiefly the intellectuals, the middle class, the more race-conscious professionals, and the industrial workers—not the sharecroppers and those on relief. The lower-strata, darker-skinned, alienated Negroes have turned not to the NAACP but to resurgent black nationalism in recent years. Assuming organized expression chiefly through the Black Muslims, black nationalism has created quite a stir in Negro communities. It embodies anger without direction, ritual without substance; it expresses resentment without specifying any clear means of resolution. American black nationalism does not contain the kind of stuff from which a large, virile, permanent racial movement can easily be built. Neither the Communist Party nor the NAACP can hope realistically to refocus the perspectives of its adherents. Neither can afford to ignore them, however.

Although the limits within which the NAACP had to act were here and there tightened, new areas were opened, and the range of organizational choices was increased; but lower-strata Negroes could rarely express their discontent except in indirect, white-sanctioned ways. Increasingly the party found that its racial doctrines could be preserved only by attributing their momentary failure to machinations of evil middle-class Negroes. It was precisely the middle-class Negroes and organizations such as the Association that knew the alternatives and had the skills to articulate their own and the race's grievances. They were more competent and had a wider range of choice than did lower-strata Negroes. Usually the latter were able to act effectively only when the middle class itself spurred them into specific protest efforts.

However, William Z. Foster and the other members of the "hard line" faction within the party were not disposed at that time to make any substantial revisions in the party's version of the Negro question and the role of the NAACP. That was to come later. Writing "Notes on the Struggle for Negro Rights," Foster defended the earlier position he had taken and claimed that the reformist organizations had received undeserved credit for advancing Negro rights:

During the several years past, especially in the war and post-war period, there has been a marked increase in the influence of bourgeois and social-reformist leaders among the Negro workers and other sections of the Negro people. Various factors have contributed to this—especially the illusions connected with the current false, war-made prosperity, which have also cultivated reformist influences in the trade union movement. But a powerful and special element operating to strengthen Negro reformism, and one that must not be ignored, is precisely the fact that government for international policy reasons . . . in making some concessions to the Negro people, has done so through the instrumentality of the reformists. Consequently, the NAACP and other organizations with reformists at their head have been enabled to profit hugely in prestige and leadership. These elements are thus getting credit for victories for which they are at best responsible only to a limited degree.[50]

There was some truth in this observation, for postwar developments in the international sphere made the American government more responsive to Negro aspirations at home. However, Foster's position was at variance with earlier recognition by the party that the NAACP was the foremost organization of Negro protest and had succeeded on its own, through the very reformist leaders he criticized.

Even if Foster depreciated the capabilities of NAACP leaders, he still proposed to work with the organization if he could:

Now, however, we face a quite different situation with the Northern Negro workers members en masse of the trade unions

[50] William Z. Foster, "Notes on the Struggle for Negro Rights," *Political Affairs*, XXXIV (May, 1955), 38–39.

—both A.F. of L. and C.I.O.—with their building of the N.A.A.C.P.
into a mass body, with their playing an increasingly important
role in the Democratic Party, and with their entering into many
other types of mass organizations from which they had hitherto
been barred. Obviously, in such a situation it is our task to base
our Negro work upon these mass organizations. A further special
consideration to this end is the fact that with the heavy government persecution of the Communist Party and all other Left and
progressive organizations, the need is all the greater to ally our-
selves closely with the masses in their organizations.[51]

Since the party failed to build a Negro following of its own,
Foster insisted that it must use the NAACP and other organizations with large Negro memberships. However, he did not
indicate how this was to be done. He was long on exhortation
and short on specific suggestion. But while Communists were
to "bore from within" the NAACP, they were warned:

In building the national solidarity of the Negro people we must
also keep in mind and always work on two fronts. That is we
must fight against the Rightist danger of tailing after the Negro
bourgeoisie, and also against the sectarian danger of isolating our-
selves from the masses through ill-advised "Left centers" and
other "Leftist" practices.[52]

The proposal required an almost impossible balancing act; it
is not surprising that Foster and his followers were unable to
walk the wire with aplomb. The task was made no easier by
the fact that in this period, with the party disintegrating and
the members confused and breaking up into factions, no clear
definitions of "Rightist . . . tailing" and left "sectarian danger" informed the behavior of Communists in their labors.

By the middle 1950's the NAACP, without necessarily intend-
ing to do so, had developed a near monopoly on organized
Negro protest in the United States. Its leaders were widely

[51] *Ibid.*, p. 40.   [52] *Ibid.*, p. 42.

recognized as spokesmen for Negroes on matters of public policies and race relations. Its methods were generally accepted as being among the most effective for securing racial rights. During the second half of the decade its hard-won position was to be challenged, but not by the Communists and their sympathizers.

Organizationally, too, the NAACP had fared well during the first postwar decade. Although it had fewer members than at the wartime peak in 1945, it had not suffered the drastic losses which came after World War I. Nevertheless, it was not growing so fast or so solidly as some of its Board members and national staff had expected after the war. In 1956 the NAACP had 350,000 dues-paying members; its gross income exceeded $800,000, which was almost twice the amount available to finance activities of the national organization in 1953. Circulation of *Crisis*, the official publication, had increased to more than 64,000; the magazine was widely read outside the organization, particularly by government officials and by members of other action groups. Local branches in 1956 numbered more than 1,200, but the problem of keeping them active was a continuing one. These figures reflected stability; the NAACP seemed to have developed a momentum that would carry it forward indefinitely. Some national officials expressed the belief that the Association could obtain a million followers within a few years.

In contrast the Communist Party continued to decline and even the most optimistic die-hards remaining in the organization saw little real hope of being able to reverse the trend. Even as the party was being overwhelmed by outside forces, its members were involved in a prolonged internal conflict in which advocates of "hard" and "soft" policies in the post-Stalin era battled each other for control of the dwindling apparatus and resources of the organization. That struggle, which reached a climax in late 1957, left the party with probably not more than ten thousand members, less than a thousand of whom were Negroes. Financially the party was greatly weakened, no longer being able to tap sources of funds in the left-wing unions or among ethnic and nationality groups. It was forced to reduce greatly the size and number of its publications. Its efforts to offset its general losses by recruiting Negroes did not pay off.

Since 1956 the NAACP has faced many challenges, few of which have come from the Communists. Particularly important have been the challenges presented by organized white segregationists, Negro nationalists, separatists, and direct actionists, especially in the southern states. Organizations such as the White Citizens Councils, the Nation of Islam (Black Muslims), the Southern Christian Leadership Conference, and the Congress of Racial Equality figure too prominently in the NAACP's calculations for the Communist Party and its racial fronts to be given much thought. Although an examination of the NAACP's response to the new movements is a tempting possibility, it does not fall within the scope of this study.

In 1957 NAACP membership was down to 281,000, a loss of almost 70,000 from the previous year. Its gross income, however, had increased to $962,000, with intensive special drives offsetting losses from dues. Circulation of *Crisis* fell to 62,000. During 1958 membership rose to 305,000 and national income to slightly more than a million dollars. During 1959 there was a further growth in membership, with more than 334,000 members reported in December. During the same year circulation of *Crisis* increased to over 75,000, more than twice the number of five years before. The following year brought another rise to 386,000 members, which approximated the wartime peak year of 1945. Gains continued during 1961, although the rate of growth was slower. In December of 1961 the NAACP listed 388,000 dues payers, and it appeared that the organization might have weathered its membership fluctuation problems. However, a preliminary report to the 1962 convention in Atlanta in July, 1962, indicated a steep decline in membership from the previous high.

The ups and downs in NAACP membership are a product of many forces which have been at play both within and outside the organization. Although a detailed exploration of those forces lies outside this study, since the party was not among them, it is worth noting that the strenuous attacks upon the Association by southern states—some of which demanded membership lists—took their toll, as did competition from the newer forms of protest.

During the late fifties and early sixties the CP has been preoccupied with peace and disarmament. In its new "united front for peace" it has taken a salient philosophical turn on the Negro question; it has at long last abandoned "self-determination in the Black Belt" as its ultimate goal for American Negroes.

The seventeenth national convention of the CPUSA in December, 1959, repudiated the old slogan and adopted full integration as the final end. For several months prior to the meeting there was considerable discussion of a draft resolution on the Negro question in party publications and at club meetings. Prepared by the Foster faction, which was then in firm control of the organization, the resolution conceded that although Negroes were an especially oppressed segment of American society, they did not by virtue of that fact constitute a nation. The resolution committed the party to an active concern with specific problems confronting Negroes; it noted that there were many "progressive" forces at play in American Negro life and a variety of racial organizations, from trade-unions to fraternal lodges, through which the Negro's struggles could be carried on. The NAACP was admitted to be "the major organization of the Negro people's movement engaged in the fight for full freedom." [53]

The Communists still insisted, however, that the NAACP had serious limitations and should be criticized and guided by those with a more fundamental understanding of history and of race relations.

[53] "On the Negro Question in the United States," resolution adopted at the 17th National Convention, Communist Party, United States, December, 1959, in *Political Affairs*, XXXIX (Feb., 1960), 44–57.

VII

Retrospect and Perspective

IDEOLOGY in the sense of a preoccupation with class differences and class perspectives is moribund in mid-century America; indeed, in the whole Western world. The performance of democratic capitalism, with its welfare state modifications, has been, despite its many faults and limitations, so impressive as to cut the heart from radical reform movements. American society, with all its frailties, offers to its members such attractive goods in the form of material wealth, mobility, opportunity, and personal freedom that few Americans are inclined to shop elsewhere; the principal goal of Negroes and other traditionally underprivileged groups has been to get into the supermarket rather than to burn it down.

The NAACP has swum with the mainstream of American life during the past twenty years. The Communist Party has not. It is difficult to build a mass movement, particularly in the United States, on frankly revolutionary aims. During periods of crisis, when the very foundations of the existing order are called into question, radical protest may mushroom. Over the long pull, however, "the masses" in a stable society, no matter how disaffected they may be, are likely to drift away from radical movements unless the movements can provide some immediately tangible results; but immediate results can be achieved only within, and by compromise with, the existing order—and therein lies trouble. For if people get something, they are apt to want more, and a system which provides a steady stream of concessions is likely to recruit friends rather than reinforce enemies. Further, the very process of winning concessions from the established order encoils the radical movement in the existing system. Thus the classic dilemma of the revolutionary labor leader: he needs to build a mass movement of workers to overthrow capitalism; but the overthrow takes time, and meanwhile the ardor of his recruits is hard to sustain unless they see some results; he therefore builds a union to wring a few interim concessions from the employer; soon he finds himself necessarily concerned about the health of the enterprise, for only by keeping it profitable can he continue to deliver wage increases and other gains to his members, who are in the meantime succumbing to *embourgeoisement* by virtue of the gains.[1]

The Communist Party found it difficult to recruit American Negroes during periods when it frankly stated its ultimate ends in revolutionary language. At other times, when the party line soft-pedaled radical talk and emphasized immediate ameliorative measures, the leadership often was uncomfortable with the fact that its short-run programs were at cross-purposes with the ultimate, overriding goal: overthrow of capitalism. Seriously to pursue redress of the Negro's grievances through the courts entails an implicit acknowledgment that a capitalist judiciary can administer justice. To seek legislation against lynching or poll taxes implies that a capitalistic congress can be responsive to proletarian and peasant pressures, a direct contradiction of the Communist thesis that government is inherently a creature of and subservient to the ruling class. To march on the White House for an executive order eliminat-

---

[1] Jane Cassels Record, "Ideologies and Trade Union Leadership" (unpublished Ph.D. dissertation, University of California, Berkeley, 1954).

ing discrimination in defense jobs implies that a capitalistic president can be other than an instrument of Wall Street imperialists and bigoted southern planters. Furthermore, if the judiciary, the congress, and the executive do prove responsive, the reform movement finds itself with an equity in their survival; for only if the existing institutions are protected can they continue to serve the immediate interests of the reformers.

The dilemma has split the party ranks time and again. "Right deviationists" have urged a program of ameliorative reform, in cooperation with the NAACP and other indigenous racial groups, as the only way to build a Negro following. "Left sectarians," on the other hand, have insisted that what few "handouts" the capitalistic system might grudgingly give Negroes would only entrap them in the system and divert them from their ultimate revolutionary mission. The party program has vacillated between the two extremes—or sought some shaky ground in the middle. An example of the comrades' attempts to follow an untenable medial course is their behavior in the Scottsboro case, for which they hired one of the most famous defense lawyers in the country to pursue the matter through the existing court structure while at the same time they denounced the American judiciary as incapable of serving justice. Another example is the ambivalent attitude toward the NAACP. Because of the Association's successes in the legal and political spheres, and its consequent rising prestige in the Negro community, the party could ill afford to ignore or spurn it completely; yet ideologically hardened Communists could scarcely be expected to look with enthusiasm upon the middle-class leadership and orientation of the NAACP. So in medial periods the party sat on the fence, damning the Association with faint praise or scoffing at its programs while simultaneously trying to build Negro fronts with the same stated purposes that the Association was embracing with notable success.

The gradualist reformer, whose purpose is to ameliorate

rather than to uproot the established order, also has methodological problems. Shall he try to employ the state as an instrument of social reform or rely exclusively on direct action; that is, shall he organize his followers as citizens or as workers and consumers? If he attempts to use the state, shall he emphasize the judicial or the political approach?

The early American Federation of Labor, disenchanted with the state as an agent of reform because hard-won labor legislation had been negated time and time again by a hostile nineteenth-century judiciary, developed a strong voluntaristic bent, relying almost exclusively on such direct-action techniques as the strike and the boycott. The NAACP, a product of the twentieth century, has found American courts more accommodative of social change; indeed, the judiciary, particularly during the past decade, has outstripped Congress as an agent of reform in the civil rights field.

The NAACP has organized Negroes primarily as citizens rather than as workers or consumers. It was to the small colored middle class—the Talented Tenth—that it originally appealed and that answered its call. Since its members were few and scattered and included virtually no industrial workers, the Association almost inevitably chose to work through the state rather than through the strike and the boycott. Because so few Negroes had the vote and because there already existed in the American Constitution and in much statutory law a sanction of the very equality which colored people yearned for, it was natural for the Association to place chief stress on judicial rather than political efforts in its first decades: if the existing legal framework contains the relief which reformers seek, the problem is one of enforcement; if it does not, the problem is one of legislative enactment. The NAACP asked the courts to interpret and enforce the first fifteen amendments to the United States Constitution—together with other law, including the southern states' "separate but equal" statutes—so as to give Negroes the right to vote in white primaries, the right to ride interstate trains unsegregated, the right to attend state-supported "white" graduate schools if no institutions of equivalent quality had been established for Negroes.

As more and more Negroes migrated from the South and gained the franchise, and as economic problems came compellingly to the forefront, the Association moved increasingly into the political field, insisting upon greater concessions from the executive and the legislative as well as from the judicial branch of government. Of the White House and of Congress the NAACP eventually demanded executive orders and legislation not merely to ensure the physical safety of Negroes—for example, a law making lynching a federal crime—but also to grant them equal rights in the voting booth, on the job, in the schools, and elsewhere. As Negroes became more militant and the white community became more enlightened and law-abiding, the Association revised its gradualism upward, seizing upon the Supreme Court's call for "a prompt and reasonable start" and "all deliberate speed" in the struggle for full equality. Instead of hacking away at only the weakest links in the chains which bound them, in the hope that the bonds could be loosened a bit decade by decade, the slogan of the 1950's became "completely free by '63."

So preoccupied was the Association with the instruments for winning *de jure* desegregation that it neglected to build an equivalent apparatus for winning *de facto* desegregation once the laws had been passed or the Supreme Court had spoken. The NAACP's failure to develop imaginative new ways of dealing with a recalcitrant South in the late 1950's handed the initiative to the Congress of Racial Equality (CORE), the Southern Christian Leadership Conference (SCLC) headed by Dr. Martin Luther King, and the Student Non-violent Coordinating Committee (SNCC). Not that NAACP leaders were unaware of the Negro's new consumer power; they were merely slow to seize upon it as a complementary weapon to political and judicial instruments.

Why? One reason was the usual degree of inflexibility which characterizes stable, successful institutions; moreover, the resources of the national office and local branches were already overstrained by the magnitude of the judicial fight; but not to be overlooked was the NAACP's dearth of close contact with college students and lower-class colored folk, especially in the South, a circumstance which may have led the Association, along with white southerners, to underestimate the militancy and courage of the ordinary Negro. The unity and staying power of the Montgomery colored community during the bus boycott were startling phenomena. The large number of Negroes who came forward to sign their names to school integration petitions in little towns all over the rural South—in the face of almost certain economic reprisal, which often meant losing jobs or credit—was unmistakable evidence of grass-roots dissidence. Furthermore, the effectiveness of the boycotts at Montgomery and Tuskegee, of the sit-ins at Jacksonville and Atlanta, of the freedom rides through Georgia and South Carolina, was a lesson spelled plainly for all to see. The white South squirmed and lamented and threatened; but it gave in, inch by inch, sometimes dramatically, under the economic pressure and moral suasion of direct-action techniques —with a surprisingly small amount of physical violence, especially outside Mississippi and Alabama.

Whereas a tedious, expensive legal battle sometimes yielded, after four or five years, the admission of one or two Negroes to a previously all-white high school, a spontaneous sit-in which lasted only a few weeks and required virtually no funds often resulted in the desegregation of a whole group of lunch counters. The Young Turks had found a way not only to use the Negro's bargaining power as a consumer but also to tap the innate decency and courtesy of the white southerner; after all, white southerners, too, are nurtured in the American equalitarian tradition, and the conspicuity of the sit-ins made flesh the conflict between ethic and practice.[2]

Not for a moment did the sit-in organizers question the overriding importance of the NAACP's legal victories; young Negroes merely asked whether the legal approach is sufficient —or fast enough. The direct actionists look upon their methods as complementary to, not competitive with, judicial and political means—as subsidiaries to, rather than as replacements for, the older approaches.

One of the salient aspects of racial protest in the past few years is the apparent need of the Negro rank-and-filer to experience a feeling of *involvement*. Direct-action methods meet that need. Everyone cannot be a plaintiff in a school case or a franchise suit. However, everyone can march, or boycott buses, or sit down in a white waiting room. Negroes marching down the streets of Albany, Georgia, in the deepest of the Deep South, following Martin Luther King to the courthouse to kneel and pray for the right to vote and to enjoy the other privileges of American citizenship must have had a sense of involvement that they scarcely could attain from contributing a few dollars to the NAACP legal fund—especially since the Albany police were on hand to arrest them for blocking traffic.[3]

Social protest movements can be classified according to differences in goal or in method. The Garvey Movement of the 1920's and the Black Muslims today are expressions of a desire not to overthrow American society but to separate from it. The Communists generally have sought not to separate from but to supplant it, though they long urged separation upon the

[2] SRC, "The Student Protest Movement, Winter 1960," special report, Atlanta, Feb., 1960, mimeo.

[3] SRC, "Albany," special report by Howard Zinn, Atlanta, Jan., 1962, mimeo.

American Negro. The NAACP and the direct actionists want neither to separate from nor to supplant American society but to become a part of it on equal terms. In pursuing that goal the methods of the NAACP and the direct-action groups are different in emphasis but are not antipathetical. There is nothing in the nonviolent character of the techniques employed by CORE and the other groups (in contrast to an earlier direct-action movement on the American scene, the IWW, which advocated sabotage and other forms of violence) that clashes with the legalism of the Association. That fact has made it easy for the NAACP, CORE, SCLC, and SNCC to work together more or less harmoniously.

When the first sit-ins occurred, many of the old guard in southern NAACP branches took a jaundiced view of them: "That's the wrong way to go about things, and the students are going to jeopardize the whole struggle." The gallantry of the young upstarts, however, together with their successes soon brought the "older heads" around, and most NAACP branches fell in behind the students and Dr. King.[4] Because of a basic compatibility of goal and method, "united front" for those indigenous Negro protest organizations assumes a semantical precision it could never attain for cooperation between the NAACP and the CPUSA, even when the party line was at its most conciliatory.

Thus the mainstream of racial dissidence as the United States pursues the seventh decade of the twentieth century is unquestionably integrationist. The freshet of radicalism has virtually dried up; separatism is a brackish slough. Even the party at long last, after thirty-five years, has given up its separatist scheme for colored folk. Since Negroes are no longer concentrated in the Black Belt, a "Negro nation" no longer makes sense geographically; it never made sense culturally or psy-

[4] Paul Jacobs, "The NAACP's New Decision," *New Republic*, July 16, 1958, p. 9, describes the NAACP dilemma.

chologically. The American black man severed his African roots in the dim past. Even his physical appearance, because of miscegenation and acculturation, has undergone transformation. After traveling abroad, Carl Rowan, Richard Wright, and other Negro Americans have reported their unexpected sense of alienation from Africans and Asians. Although moved by the struggles of colored peoples to throw off the yoke of white imperialism and to establish independent national states, the American Negro is an American. In his thirst for cultural assimilation he follows the traditional pattern of American ethnic minorities, a pattern which has deprived American society of a refreshing cultural diversity.

Had the offerings of the American economic system been less attractive, or had the political structure been less accommodative of the aspirations of disfranchised minorities to be free and equal, Negro movements might have taken a more radical turn. But the institutional environment and the temper of the times underwrote the success of moderate, gradualist, integrationist reformers who pushed at the gates hard enough, just as the institutional environment and the temper of the times underwrote the failure of the Communists and other radical reformers.

What is ahead for the cp in its "Negro work?" Probably continued limbo, barring the kind of major default by the existing political and economic system at home or the kind of world triumph of communism that is difficult to conceive in the early 1960's.

And what is ahead for the NAACP? In a sense the Association is working itself out of a job. Since its single purpose is to eliminate racial barriers, once the barriers are down there will be no *raison d'être* for an NAACP; indeed, once that glorious day arrives, continued organization of Negroes *qua* Negroes would negate what the Association has been striving for from the beginning. Negroes who dislike aspects of American society other than racial discrimination will continue to work through protest movements other than the NAACP; and it is to be hoped that with racialism behind and full acceptance won, there will come a relaxation on the part of Negroes about books and plays and movies which portray a colored man in an unfavorable light, for sophistication in such matters is the ultimate gauge of mature citizenship and full equality.

Of course, the interracial millennium is not likely to begin next year or next decade. Meanwhile the Association, if it remains flexible and hard-pressing, will probably continue to be the premier Negro protest movement in the United States, an object of study for social scientists examining the major social movements of the present era. The Communist Party, at least for the time being, belongs to the historians.

Index